Big Fat Cat vs. MR. JONES

Takahiko Mukoyama
Tetsuo Takashima
with studio ET CETERA

GENTOSHA

PREVIOUSLY IN THE BIG FAT CAT SERIES
〜これまでの BIG FAT CAT シリーズ〜

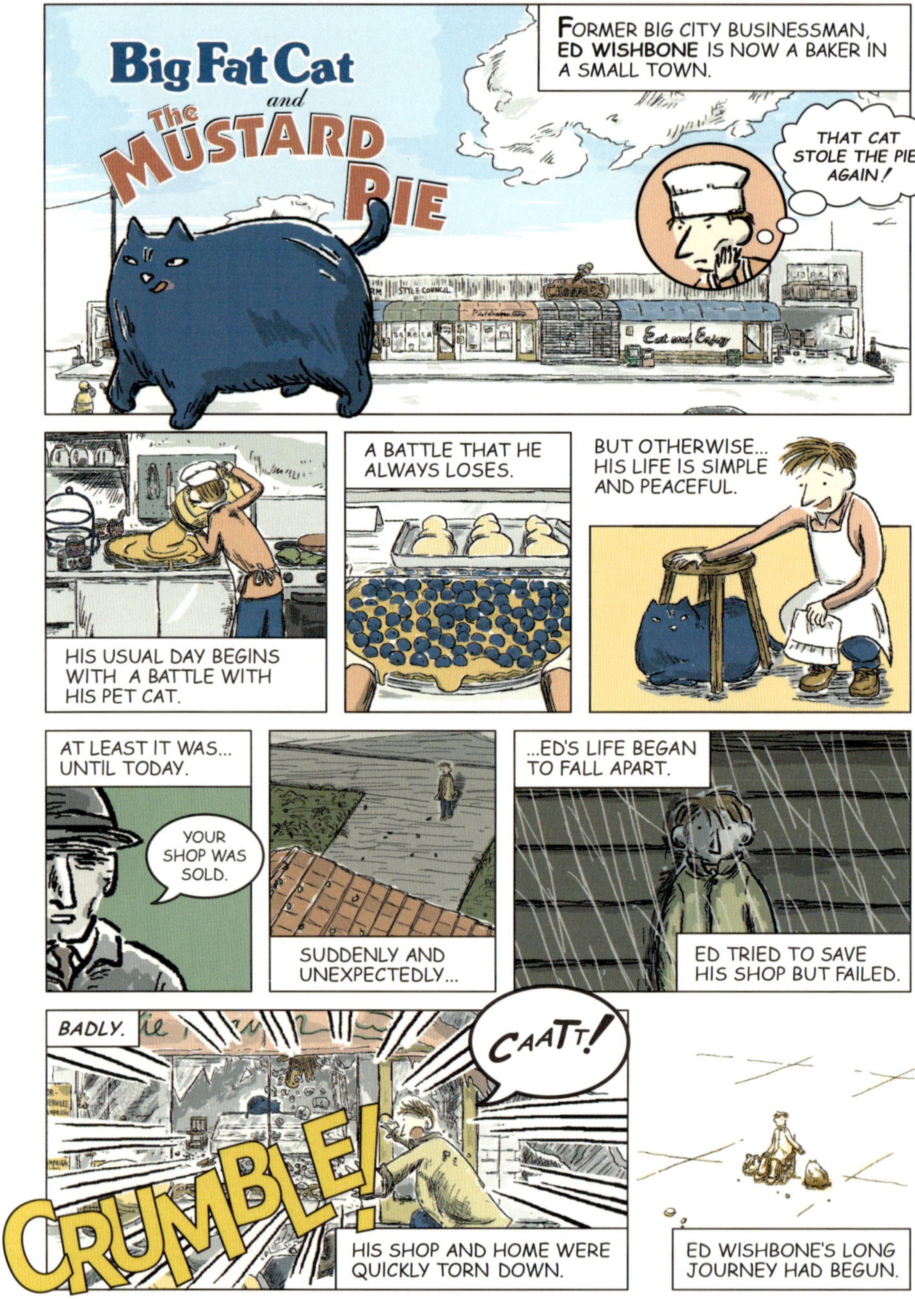

Big Fat Cat and the GHOST AVENUE

A COLD WINTER NIGHT.

ED WISHBONE IS ALONE, SEARCHING FOR HIS CAT.

HE FALLS ASLEEP IN AN OLD DESERTED GHOST STREET UPTOWN.

AND IS AWAKENED BY 'GHOSTS.'

WOOOOOo

GEORGE

THE 'GHOSTS' OF GHOST AVENUE.

BEE JEES

PEOPLE FORGOTTEN FROM THE REAL WORLD.

PEOPLE WHO HAVE NOT HAD A SLICE OF PIE IN MANY YEARS.

PEOPLE WITH LIVES MUCH WORSE THAN ED COULD EVER IMAGINE.

FRANK

WILLY

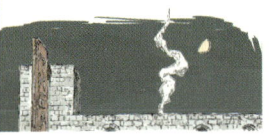

ED WISHBONE LEARNED A LESSON THAT WINTER NIGHT.

THANK YOU.

LIFE IS NOT A SWEET PIE.

SOMETIMES, IT'S UNFAIR.

BUT OTHER TIMES, IT'S FAIR...

AND YOU JUST HAVE TO EAT THE PIE YOU GET.

HA HA HA!

SO EAT IT.

SEASON 1
THE END

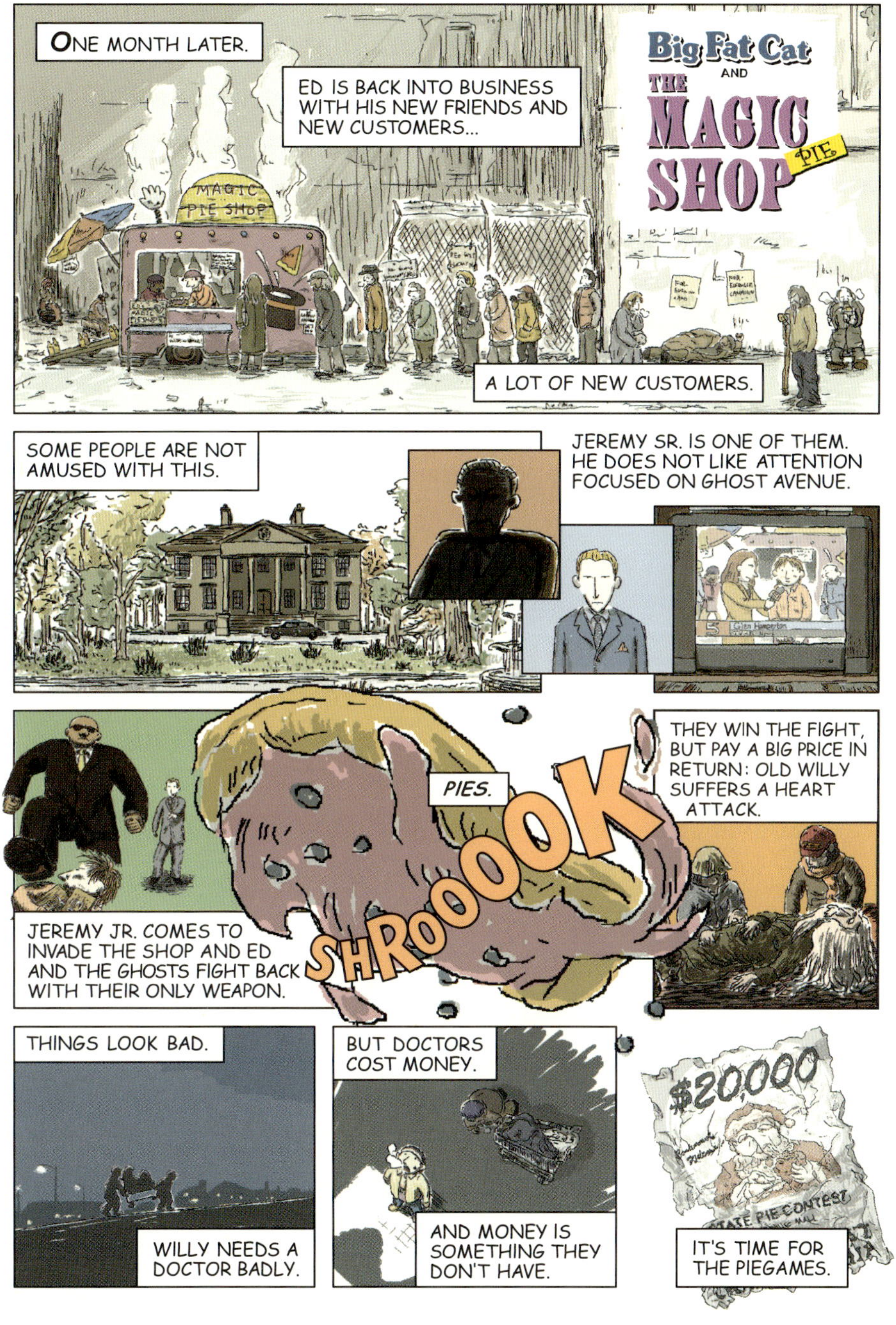

"George..."

"George..."

"It's morning."

BFC BOOKS SERIES / PART 5 (season 2)

"Oh... Ed. Good morning," George said. He rubbed his sleepy eye with one hand as he got up.

The sun was barely up in the sky. Fresh and crisp air filled the dawn of Everville's older streets. It was seven o'clock in the morning — the beginning of a new day.

After a moment of recovery, George smiled and pointed before him.

"There's your stuff. Good and ready."

In front of George, there was a pile of kitchen utensils that Ed used everyday. They were the cheapest brand at the nearby supermarket, but now they shined like silver in the morning light. Ed noticed that George's hands were all red.

"This was all I could do. But I'll be in the front row today, cheering like hell," George said.

Ed picked up his rolling pin. Yesterday, it had been an old gray color. Now it was practically new.

"George... we don't have any sandpaper. This is impossible. How did you..."

George took out a completely worn-out toothbrush. He grinned like a child.

Ed stood amazed. He couldn't imagine how many hours it would take to scrub a rolling pin with a toothbrush.

"George, this is impossible!"

"Almost," George said and smiled.

Ed touched the rolling pin with the tip of his fingers. He thought he could feel the warmth inside.

"George, you can't sit in the front row today," he said to George.

"Oh..."

A look of despair crossed George's face for a moment. But he replied quickly. He was used to this kind of treatment all his life.

"Oh... well, I know. I guess I would make a bad impression on the judges. Hey, no problem! I'll just stay in the back and keep..."

Ed held the contest flier out to George. An entry form and a list of rules were printed on the back. Ed pointed to one particular rule.

"It says here, I can bring one assistant." Ed smiled. "You're going to be that assistant."

"Say what?" George replied. His face turned red as he looked up at Ed. He immediately shook his head.

"No way, man. You don't want me! Uh-un! I'll just mess things up. I always do."

"I went to the Mall yesterday and registered. You already are my assistant, George. I need your help," Ed said.

George stared at Ed.

The morning sun, now higher in the sky, gave bright light onto the old neighborhood. Most of the others were still asleep and the street was quiet.

"Are you sure?" George asked.

Ed nodded.

"Nobody ever asked for my help. Ed... you're... you're so..." George said in a trembling voice.

"Come on, George," Ed said, looking up into the blue sky. It seemed to be the start of a really nice winter day. "Let's get going."

"You're damn right, we're going!" George shouted as he stood up in pride.

And with that, the day began.

"AAAAND IT'S A GREAT NEW DAY!! The balloons are up! We're on top of the New Everville Mall this morning, reporting live from the annual State Pie Festival! This is Glen Hamperton, bringing you the excitement below — live on the morning news!"

"Today, eighteen shops and individuals enter the pie contest to find the best pie in the state. This year's main sponsor Wilson Artwill, the owner of the New Everville Mall, has prepared a huge cash prize of twenty thousand dollars and a free space for a shop in his Food Court.

"The rules are simple. Contestants have two hours to bake the best pie. They can use any ingredients they choose, but each contestant can have only one assistant for help.

"At the end of two hours, all the pies will be presented to the judges. Each contestant will introduce their pie in the way they wish. After tasting all eighteen pies, the judges will each vote for the best pie. The numbers will be added up, and the single contestant with the highest score will win the 'GOLDEN CRUST' trophy along with the prize money and the store space! The excitement is heating up as the time draws near for the battle of the pies to begin!

"WELCOME TO THE PIEGAMES!

"I'm Glen Hamperton reporting live from the air above Everville! See you later, folks!"

The street was still quiet.

It was nearly nine a.m., but in Ghost Avenue, morning was longer than any other place. Ed crept through the piles of junk inside the Old Everville Cinema, heading towards the campfire in the middle. BeeJees was half-asleep near the fire. Besides him, Willy lay on a fake bed that Ed and the others had made.

Willy hadn't woken up once in two days. He was still alive, but barely.

"Willy," Ed whispered.

But Willy didn't react.

"I have to go. But I'll be back soon. Then we'll get you to a hospital, okay?" Ed said.

The light of the fire fell on Willy's face. Sometimes the flickering light made Willy seem to move a little. Unfortunately, it was always only a trick of the eye.

A faint cracking sound broke the silence. Ed looked behind him and found BeeJees awake, slumped against an old sign. BeeJees was holding a fortune cookie which he had just cracked open in his hands.

"BeeJees, I'm sorry about what I said the other night," Ed said to BeeJees. "I... I'm really sorry."

BeeJees scratched his head, frowned, and looked down. He pulled out a thin piece of paper from inside the fortune cookie. After a long pause, he read from the paper in a flat voice.

"There are chances, and there are consequences."

BeeJees shook his head and chuckled. "What the hell does that mean?"

He dropped the paper and cookie on the floor and crushed them under his foot.

"The Prof loved these things. The Chinese store downtown used to give him cookies that had expired. He cracked one open every morning and read the paper inside. It always said something stupid like that. He just read them and smiled. That crazy old bastard."

BeeJees laughed weakly.

Ed had taken his bandanna out and was folding it in half. He wrapped it around his head and tied it in the back. Right then, Frank came rolling around the corner in his toy wagon. He said "Howdy" to Ed and waved at him. Ed waved back.

"You really think you can win this contest?" BeeJees asked.

Ed held a solemn expression on his face, but his eyes were determined. BeeJees cracked open another fortune cookie. This time, he crushed it without even reading the paper inside.

"Do you at least have a plan? Everyone else in the contest is a professional. You're just a guy from a small town. What do you plan to do?"

"What Willy told me." Ed reached for his bag as he said, "Try to be a baker."

Ed started for the door, looking back at Willy one last time. Willy slept on, cuddled in a pile of dirty rags.

At least he deserves a better bed, Ed thought. It made him want to cry. But there was no time for crying.

"Watch the cat for me, Frank. It's going to be a disaster if the cat finds out where I'm going," Ed said to Frank.

"Ai-ya!" Frank replied.

George was waiting by the doors, dressed in his best outfit. It was a cheap tuxedo. He looked like a boy waiting for his first day of Sunday school. This made Ed smile again.

"Ed," BeeJees suddenly shouted. Ed looked back as BeeJees threw him a fortune cookie. Ed caught the cookie with both hands.

"Take Willy with you," BeeJees said.

Ed raised his eyes and nodded once.

It was time to go.

"This is Glen Hamperton, reporting from outside the main tent of the State Pie Festival. The time is now ten a.m. and contestants should be here any minute now... and YES! Here they come! This year's pie warriors!

"Leading the group is the two-time contest winner 'Brown Butters' — now at four locations around the state. Their famous 'Brown Butter Vanilla Double Crust' has been the number one best-selling pie for more than fifteen years!

"Right behind them are the 'Buffi Brothers.' Combining traditional Italian cuisine with the art of pie baking, they have created a revolution in the history of pies. Their specialty is the 'Pepperoni Pie' with cheese, tomato sauce, pasta and a whole lot of sliced pepperoni!

"And... oh my God... what is that blue smoke back there!? Has there been an accident? No, wait... that music, that rhythm... Yes, everyone! This is the one you've been waiting for! The crowd is going crazy! We now present you, the one and only... ZOMBIE PIES!!

"It's the strangest pie shop in the history of strange pie shops! The Pie God himself, Jeremy Lightfoot Jr., and the colorful Zombie Pies trailer are now entering the tent. Their horrifying mascot, 'The Gravedigger,' stalks the grounds while the 'Grim Zombies' are scaring kids who unfortunately got in their way! Already condemned by twenty-one school boards, Zombie Pies is nevertheless the most famous pie shop in ten surrounding states!

"Reporting live from the entrance of the PIEGAMES, I'm Glen Hamperton! The battle is about to begin!!"

Meanwhile... at the main gate.

"Oh my God..." George said, and forgot to shut his mouth. "Ed, I think this is a big mistake."

George stared at the fabulous Zombie Pies trailer truck as it entered the tent, his mouth wide open.

Ed was also frozen there at the gate of the pie festival. He scanned the festival grounds with both his eyes, surprised at how big the event was. There was a Ferris wheel standing at the far side, along with several other carnival rides.

　Countless booths selling every kind of pie on earth were lined back to back down the main area. People of all ages were everywhere. There were balloons, flags, and other multi-colored decorations all around.

　Before arriving at the festival grounds, Ed had imagined an auditorium with fifty or a hundred people. He couldn't have been more wrong.

　　Ed gulped.

George looked at Ed with big, frightened-puppy eyes. George was probably the only person in the whole festival grounds wearing a tuxedo, except for the stuffed bear on the counter of a nearby booth.

"This is crazy, man. BeeJees is right. We're waaaay out of our league here. Let's go home."

George turned to leave, but Ed grabbed his arm.

"George, we've got no choice."

"I know, man. But I'm scared."

"Me too," Ed said, and started walking towards the main tent. George stood there alone at the gate for a moment. But when people nearby began to look at him suspiciously, he started to run after Ed — but fell because of his shaking legs. He got up and continued to run.

"Ed! Hey! Wait up! Ed!"

Unnoticed by either of them, a dark shadow crouched by the gate silently, watching everything.

"Thank you, Glen. And now, this is your host Robert R. Silverman from inside the main tent. Almost all of the contestants have finished setting up their kitchens here on the battleground. All we can do is wait for the clock to... oops, someone just came into the tent from the contestant's side.

"Hey, mister, you've got the wrong gate! But, oh... wait a minute... am I dreaming this, or... Good Lord! This man seems to be our last contestant!

"He has now stopped at booth five. Let's see... his name seems to be 'Ed Wishbone.' Funny, the name sort of rings a bell. Where have I heard... Holy cow! *It's the baker from Ghost Avenue!* We've all seen him on the six o'clock news! My God, I don't want to be rude here, but Ed, man, maybe you should open your eyes and take a look around!

"Uh-oh... More bad news. I'm afraid Mr. Tuxedo here is Ed's assistant. I just hope that barrel he's dragging(ひきずっている) isn't what I think it is. If this is a joke, it sure seems to work, because everyone in the stands is laughing like crazy. Ladies and gentlemen, let's just hope that the judges' health is still intact(無事) when they go home tonight!"

"Holy macaroni! Is that his oven!?" Jeremy's assistant said. He was laughing and pointing at Ed as they set up the barrel oven.

George was so embarrassed that he lost his grip, and the barrel oven toppled over. The crowd went wild. Ed and George just kept on trying to balance the barrel. The crowd laughed as if they were watching a circus.

"Is he really going to enter the contest!? Man, talk about crazy people..."

"Shut up," Jeremy said. He was concentrating on checking the oven.

"But boss, you should take a look at this guy. He is totally out of his..."

Jeremy hit the top of the oven hard with his hand. The assistant stopped babbling. Jeremy was dressed in costume, but his face was dead serious. He slowly pulled his hand back and hid it behind him. It hurt.

"I said... quiet. Stop laughing, and keep your mind on your job."

The surprised assistant replied, "Yes, sir." He got back to work in a hurry.

Jeremy glanced at Ed and George with a look of disgust, then focused again on his oven. He tried to dismiss the duo from his mind, but kept remembering the taste of that pie.

An ordinary pie. *That was all.* An ordinary fruit pie. But he still couldn't forget the taste. It made him nervous.

"Okay, Wishbone. You're here," Jeremy mumbled. "Now, prove yourself."

Meanwhile behind the Zombie Pies trailer.

Billy Bob listened to his cell phone in silence. He didn't say anything. He didn't even nod. He just listened. Finally, before hanging up, he said one phrase.

"Yes, sir."

Billy Bob was standing between the trailer and the back wall where almost nobody could see him. He carefully set Mr. Jones' carrier cage down on the ground and moved away into the back alley.

A moment later, Jeremy's assistant came rushing out of the trailer. Jeremy was yelling, "Go get it and hurry!" from behind him. The assistant was so upset that he swung open the back door with all of his might. The door hit Mr. Jones' cage and knocked it over.

The carrier rolled over twice and the door of the cage sprang wide open.

Everything lay still for a while. But then, inch by inch, Mr. Jones pushed its head out and looked around. — After a brief pause, Mr. Jones hid inside the cage again.

Another minute passed. Mr. Jones decided to take a step outside again. It slowly crept out of the cage, and even more slowly, took one step, then two steps out on the ground.

It felt good. Mr. Jones took a big stretch and narrowed its eyes. It then walked over to a trailer tire, sniffed it, and rubbed a side against it. Satisfied, Mr. Jones continued walking down the alley.

It couldn't understand what was happening, but being outside of the cage was much better than being inside of it. Free space to walk around was luxurious.

So this was the world outside. The world beyond the bars.

It was so free, and...

... and it was also pretty scary.

The last time George had seen a real Santa Claus was more than thirty years ago, back in elementary school. His mom had taken all the kids to the Outside Mall one afternoon, where Santa came every winter. Back then, the Outside Mall was the coolest place a kid could go.

Now, thirty years later, a chubby Santa with a white beard and red suit was walking straight towards them.

"Ed Wishbone?" Santa Claus asked.

George turned to Ed, his eyes wide open.

"You're friends with Santa?" George asked.

Ed looked up from the table as Santa took off his beard. It was the owner of the New Mall.

"Ed Wishbone! I thought that was you!" the owner said. "I was worried after you disappeared from the clinic. Are you okay?"

Ed smiled awkwardly as he replied.

"I'm fine, sir. I'm sorry for everything. I don't really remember much about that night."

"No problem, no problem," the owner said, but the smile faded from his face. "You know, Jeremy Lightfoot's bodyguard came to my office several days after you disappeared. He had a paper with your signature on it. It said that you disclaimed all rights to the space in the Food Court. I knew the paper was suspicious, but I really had no choice but to believe it."

Ed nodded.

"So I didn't rent the space to Zombie Pies either. Instead, I saved it as the prize for the contest today. I sincerely hope you win."

"Thank you."

"I'm sorry about what happened."

"No. Don't be. It was all for the best. I..."

Just then, a bell rang throughout the main tent, signaling the start of the contest in five minutes. The owner hurriedly put his beard back on. He smiled at Ed.

"Good luck, Mr. Wishbone."

"Thank you, sir," Ed said.

The owner ran off, his fluffy cap flip-flopping with every step.

"I didn't know Santa's beard was fake," George said in an astonished face.

Ed chuckled and turned back to his table. Everything was ready and in place. The only thing now was to decide what kind of pie to make.

Ed knelt down and inspected the bags he had brought. In one bag were the ingredients for a blueberry pie. But the other bag held the ingredients for another kind of pie. Ed had not mentioned this to George.

The safe choice was blueberry. There was no doubt about it. Yet, something inside Ed kept telling him that he should enter the contest with his own pie. Not a pie borrowed from his mother's recipe book.

But that was risky. It was more than a risk. Yet...

His hand was moving slowly towards the second bag when George said,

"Damn! Willy sure would have wanted to see this!"

Ed's hand stopped a few inches from the bag.

He clenched the hand into a fist, then grabbed the bag with the blueberries in it instead.

Willy. Ed thought to himself. *Think about Willy. You have to win. No matter what.*

Moments later, the bell rang again, and all of the contestants sprang to a start. The clock tower standing in the middle of the tent turned twelve. The host was shouting in excitement. The crowd roared.

And from there on, everything became a blur. The world seemed to move in fast-forward.

The battle had begun.

An hour later, Jeremy was about to finish his crust when he noticed Billy Bob standing near Ed Wishbone's booth. Only Jeremy and a few others could have possibly spotted him. He was standing in a shadowy corner.

A bad feeling ran through Jeremy's mind as his busy hands stopped moving for a moment.

Billy Bob was checking to see if Ed Wishbone and his assistant were away from their table. — They were. Ed and George were over by the barrel oven, trying to build up a steady fire.

Before Jeremy could even think, Billy Bob stepped out. He took something from the table and replaced it with something else. It was impossible to determine what it was, but he had definitely done something to Wishbone's materials.

When Ed returned to his table a few seconds later, Billy Bob had disappeared completely, as if he had never been there.

Jeremy took off his apron (エプロン) and laid (置く) it on the table. He hurried out of the trailer and went racing through the back door. Billy Bob was just coming down the alley. Enraged (怒り狂って), Jeremy confronted (対峙する) Billy Bob head-on.

"You! What were you doing? Tell me!"

Jeremy grabbed Billy Bob by his jacket and pulled, but Billy Bob didn't move an inch. Nor did his expression change.

"Did my father tell you to do this?"

Billy Bob didn't answer.

"Damn it! I'm not going to let you and my father mess this up! I'm going to win this on my own!"

Billy Bob's cell phone rang. With one movement, Billy Bob brushed Jeremy aside and pulled his phone out. Jeremy went sprawling to the ground, hitting his elbow hard. Ignoring Jeremy, Billy Bob answered the phone. Only Billy Bob's eyes kept watching Jeremy, as if Jeremy too was a pet.

"It's done," Billy Bob said into the phone, then hung up. He walked away without any more words.

Jeremy closed his eyes in both anger and bitterness. Back in the main arena, the host continued to feed the crowd's excitement. Upbeat music rocked the thin walls. The noise all blended together, erasing all sound, including the voice of Jeremy crying.

"The clock now reads one-forty-five. Only fifteen minutes left!

"Most of the pies are already in the oven. There's a nice smell of sugar and spice in the air as I speak!

"Zombie Pies owner Jeremy Lightfoot Jr. disappeared mysteriously from his kitchen around the end of the first hour. We have no information regarding Lightfoot's disappearance, but it may be part of some secret plan.

"Meanwhile, Ed Wishbone and his assistant, now known to the audience as 'the Tux', have continued to hold the crowd's attention with their very unusual oven.

"Oops, it seems for the moment, Ed has disappeared too. But I think it's a safe guess that this has nothing to do with any secret plan."

"Wishbone!"

Ed stopped in the middle of the back alley when he heard his name. Jeremy had appeared out of the shadows behind him.

In this damp, dark corridor, all the music and excitement seemed far away, as if it came from a different world.

Jeremy was alone. He slowly took a few steps towards Ed. Ed nervously took a step back.

Jeremy Lightfoot Jr. wore a solemn face. He closed his eyes for a moment, clenched his fists, and just stood there. He seemed like he was fighting something inside of himself.

"I... uh... have to go," Ed said, and took a step back towards his booth as Jeremy opened his mouth.

"Check your pie," Jeremy said.

"What?" Ed asked.

"Your pie. I saw someone mess with your supplies when you weren't looking."

Ed stared at Jeremy.

In the quiet refuge^(避難所) of the back alley, the two young bakers really saw each other for the first time. And for some reason, it seemed like looking into a mirror. They both realized it was not a matter of money or pride or proving anything anymore. It was just about pies now.

"My pie?" Ed whispered, his face clouding^(くもる).

Jeremy nodded.

Ed glanced at the clock on the wall. There were only thirteen more minutes until time was up. If something was wrong with the pie he was baking now, there was no time to start over again.

"Go," Jeremy said.

Ed nodded. He started to run back but paused briefly only to say to Jeremy,

"Thanks."

Jeremy closed his eyes again as Ed went dashing for the door. He couldn't tell Ed who had messed with his stuff, and it hurt.

It hurt very badly.

Ghost Avenue. Same time.

Frank hurled piles of rotting magazines and pieces of wood into the fire, trying to warm up the theater. But it was still cold. The cruel coldness sneaked in through the hole in the roof, the cracks in the wall, the broken windows, and anywhere else it could.

Willy had started shaking a few minutes ago. BeeJees brought every rag he could find and wrapped them around Willy but the shaking didn't subside.

"Frank! More fire! Burn everything! Anything!" BeeJees shouted frantically.

Frank immediately took off his jacket and threw it into the fire. But it was no use.

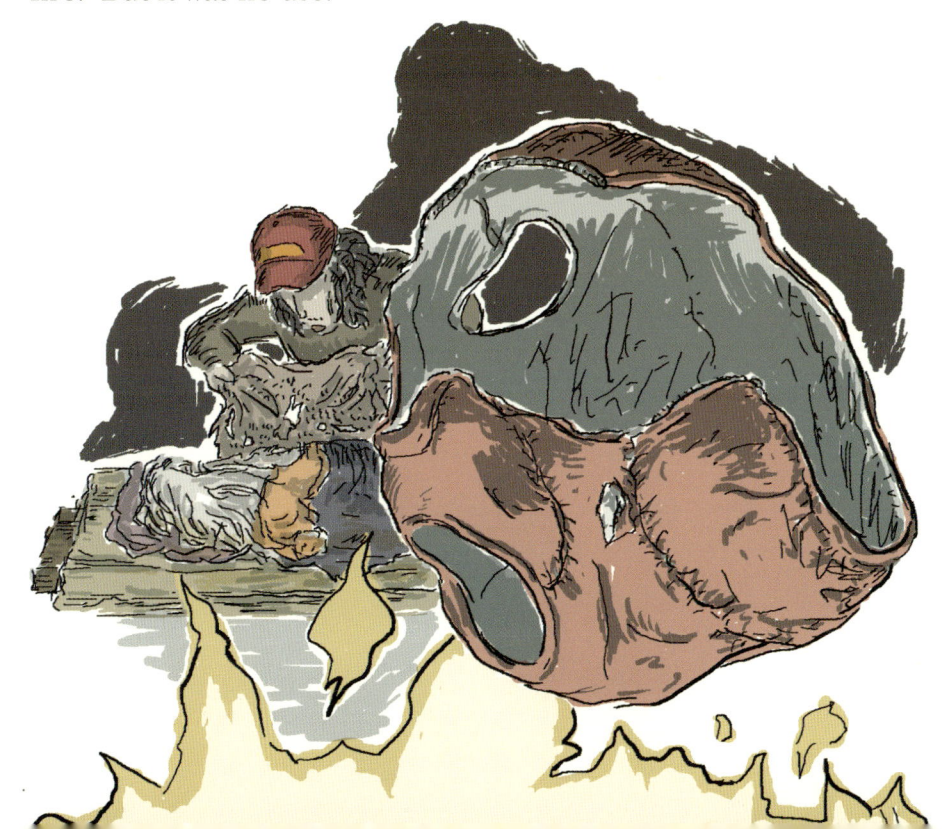

"Prof! Prof! Hang on! Stay with me, Prof! That kid will be back soon with the money! I know he will! Just hold on!"

Willy kept shaking. BeeJees, tears in his eyes, hugged Willy from top of the blankets, trying to keep him from falling off the bed. BeeJees was scared. He was so scared.

"Hurry, Ed!" BeeJees said. It sounded like a prayer. "Please hurry... Please..."

"George! The oven! Check the pies!"

George looked towards the back door. He saw Ed come running back with a hint of panic in his eyes.

The pies would be done in maybe another five minutes. He couldn't understand why Ed was in such a rush.

"Hey, man. Take it easy. Everything's fine, man."

Ed ran past George, grabbed the mitten hanging on the side of the oven, and without any hesitation, opened the oven door. A cloud of smoke rose out of the small door, making Ed and George cough. Ed knew immediately that something was terribly wrong. There shouldn't be this much smoke inside the oven. He gulped as the smoke began to clear.

As soon as he could see inside, Ed pulled a slightly burned pie out of the oven and hurried over to the table.

"Ed! What the hell are you doing!?" George shouted when he saw Ed take out a cutting knife. "That pie isn't finished yet!"

But Ed cut the pie in half. He broke off a piece of crust, dipped it in the filling, and popped it in his mouth. He tasted it for a moment and froze.

Ed said something but the applause of the audience was getting louder and George couldn't hear him.

"... other pie," Ed said again to George, but most of it was drowned out by the sound of the audience.

"Say what?" George asked close to Ed's ear.

"Get the other pie out of the oven! Fast!" Ed repeated, much louder this time.

Hearing the urgency in Ed's voice, George flew over to the oven and returned quickly with the other pie. Ed cut this one in half too, and tasted a piece of it. His reaction was almost the same. But this time, his face lost color completely.

George also took a piece of the pie and bit into it. Almost instantly, he spit it out.

"God! What the hell...?"

George turned to Ed.

"Someone did something to my stuff," Ed said.

George couldn't understand what Ed said for a moment. Then, the full horror sank in. The pies were ruined. There was no more time left.

Ed glanced at the clock tower.

Seven minutes.

The contest was in full swing. Most of the contestants were carrying finished pies from their booths to the judges' area. Ed could do nothing except stare at the two ruined pies on the table.

"Ed!" George tugged on Ed's sleeve. "C'mon, Ed! We still have time! I'll run and get anything! Just tell me what you need!"

Ed still hadn't recovered control, but he said to George in a trembling voice.

"Heat... two more cups of blueberry in a saucepan."

"Gotcha!"

George dashed away, confident that Ed knew a way to repair the pie. But he didn't. He had started scraping the filling out of the crust, but he knew it was impossible.

There was no way to make a pie in seven minutes.

TO BE CONTINUED

BFC BOOKS PRESENTS:
失われた領域を探して

「翻訳」という曖昧で不思議な世界。
その扉をくぐると、いつもは見えない世界が見えてくる。
未知の領域へいざ、出発――。

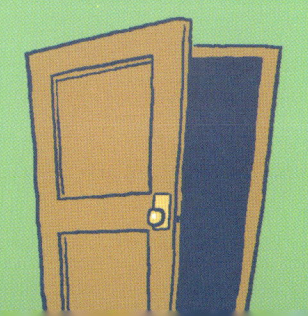

「失われた領域」

　日本の中学校、高校、そして大学の英語教育では、基本的に「翻訳する」ことが勉強の中心となっています。「英語は分からない→それなら日本語に変えよう」という発想がその元にあります。日本の英語教育で「英単語を10個覚える」ということは、「英単語10個の訳語を覚える」ことを指しています。これは英単語そのものを10個覚えるということとは、少しちがいます。

　日本での英語教育になれていると、翻訳して覚えることが外国語を学ぶ上で唯一の方法のように思えますが、決してそんなことはありません。有効な学習方法のひとつであるのは確かですが、この方法はすでに自分の国の言語をマスターしていることが前提条件になっています。国語が苦手な人や、小さな子供には不可能なやり方です。そして、この学習の仕方には致命的な弱点もあります。

　それは翻訳する際にいろいろなものが、ひそかに――でも、確実に失われてしまうことです。

　「翻訳」が100%成立するためには、英語の単語ひとつに対して、必ずそれと同じ単語（もしくは単語群）が日本語に存在する必要があります。つまり、英語と日本語の間に、完全な対応関係が成り立たなければなりません。

　でも、残念ながら、日本と欧米はまったくちがう風土、文化、宗教、歴史を持った国です。対応関係は当然ありません。それでも強引に英語を日本語に翻訳しようとした場合、そこには必ずひずみが生じてしまいます。そして、そのひずみの中へ大切なものが次々と消えて行きます。

　今回の解説は翻訳の時に生じるひずみの部分、その「失われた領域」へと一歩足を踏み入れ、外国語を学ぶことの本当の意味、そして日常生活の常識さえもくつがえしてしまう、外国語の不思議な面白さをとことん追いかけてみたいと思います。

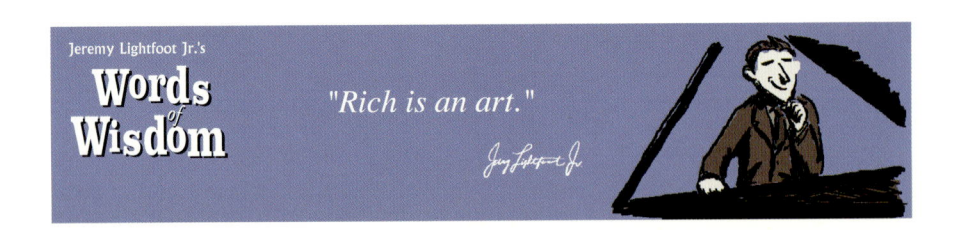

Jeremy Lightfoot Jr.'s
Words of Wisdom

"Rich is an art."

Jerry Lightfoot Jr.

さあ、それではいざ「失われた領域」へ——。

「study」を勉強する

「勉強する」。

少しいやな響きの言葉ですが、この言葉を英語に翻訳するとしたら、どんな単語が最初に頭に浮かぶでしょうか？　真っ先に出てくるのはおそらく「**study**」ではないかと思います。しかし、**study** は本当に「勉強する」という意味なのでしょうか？

日本人が「勉強する」という言葉を使う時に感じているあまりよくないイメージは、英語の **study** にはありません。**study** はなぜか「勉強する」よりも、ほんの少しだけ「かっこいい」言葉なのです。

試しに **study** を文章の中で使ってみましょう。

1. I studied English in high school.
2. I studied the crime scene.

1 の文を翻訳すると、「私は高校で英語を勉強しました」という文になります。確かに日本語の「勉強する」と同じ意味合いです。しかし、2 の文は日本語にすると「私は犯

行現場を調べました」という文になって、ずいぶんイメージが変わります。

　日本では「勉強する」という言葉には、暗記や計算をコツコツやるイメージがありますが、英語の「study」は、「研究する」や「観察する」といった広い範囲の意味を含んだ言葉なのです。

　このイメージのちがいから、小学生の勉強など、「study」というには単純すぎる作業をする場合、英語では一般的にそれを「work」と呼んでいます。一方、この work という単語は日本語に直訳すると「働く」という意味になりますが、算数のドリルをやっている子供に対して「働いている」という表現はちょっと考えられません。これは日本語の「働く」という言葉が、「報酬のために労働をする」イメージを強く持っていて、英語の「単調な作業を繰り返す」イメージの「work」とは微妙にちがっているからです。

| 勉強する | study | 働く | work |

　「勉強する」と「study」、「働く」と「work」——辞典ではイコールで結ばれていても、これらはけっこうちがう言葉です。「study」と「勉強する」が共通して持っているのは、「何らかの事柄を学んでいる」というイメージぐらいのもので、実際にやっている作業には大きな差があります。

　ややこしいので、これらの単語のちがいを分かりやすく、目に見える形にしてみましょう。

BFC JUMBLE

Unscramble the words, then collect the letters in the circle.
Unscramble once more to find the answer to the quiz!

Q: Ed has forgotten something. What?
A: The cat's ○○○○○

Big Fat Cat vs. Mr. Jones

たとえば「勉強する」という日本語が含んでいるすべての要素を青い円にしたとします。

勉強する

これに対して、英語の **study** が持っているすべての要素を黄色い円にします。

study

この二つの言葉の意味がまったく同じなら、二つの円はぴったり重なるはずですが、実際にはこんな感じでしか重なりません。

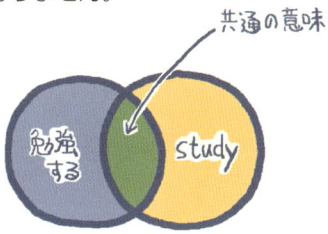

共通の意味

勉強する　study

重なった緑の部分の意味だけが共通していて、あとはまったくちがう別の言葉です。英和辞典では一応同じ意味の単語とされていても、重なっている部分が大きい単語もあれば、ほとんど重なる部分のない単語もあります。でも、円がぴったり重なる単語だけはひとつもありません。「りんご」と「**apple**」というような、ひとつの意味しかなさそうな単語でさえ、少しは円がずれてしまいます。

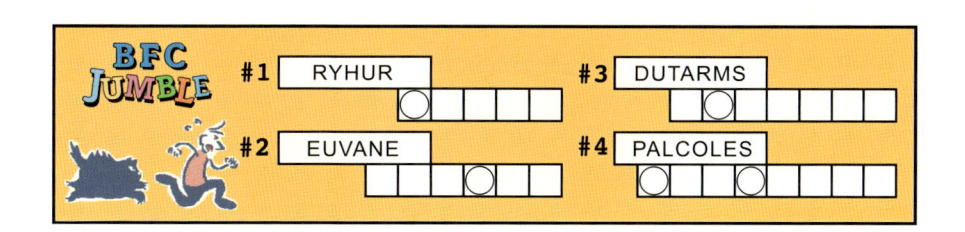

BFC JUMBLE

#1 RYHUR
#2 EUVANE
#3 DUTARMS
#4 PALCOLES

57

翻訳するというのは、この重なった緑の部分だけを取り出して、残りの部分を捨ててしまうことです。その捨てられた部分に入っていた意味やニュアンス、書き手の気持ちは翻訳された時点ですべて「失われた領域」へと消えていきます。残された表面上の意味だけで原文の思いを汲み取るのはあまりに乱暴です。

もし翻訳だけですべてが解決するなら、**result** と **consequence** のように、日本語だと同じ意味になってしまう言葉（両方とも「結果」）を欧米人が使い分けている理由が分かりません。たとえ日本語では同じ言葉に訳されるとしても、彼らにはやはりまったくちがう単語のはずですから。

笑い方の種類

ひとつ、その極端な例を紹介しましょう。「笑う」という言葉です。日本語では「笑う」というと……

これも……　　　これも……　　　そして、これも……

Big Fat Cat vs. Mr. Jones

……みんな「笑う」です。

ところが、これが英語になると、驚くほど状況が変わります。なぜなら、英語では「笑う」というひとつの動作を、こんなにたくさんの言葉に分けているからです。

laugh
声をあげて笑う

smile
笑みを浮かべる

sneer
冷ややかに笑う

smirk
悪意のある気取った笑い

giggle
くすくす笑う

chuckle
押し殺した笑い

crack up
大笑いする

ridicule
笑いものにする

jeer
笑いながらやじる

mock
（相手のまねなどをして）
からかう

Ingredients

(for the crust)
150g graham crackers
3 tablespoons soft brown sugar
1/3 cup melted butter or margarine

(for the filling)
2/3 cup sugar
1/3 cup melted butter or margarine
1 cup corn syrup
3 eggs
1/2 teaspoon salt
1 cup pecan nuts

びっくりしましたか？　でも、まだまだこんなものではありません。本当はもっとたくさんあるはずです。この中で会話に頻繁に使われるのは smile、laugh、giggle、crack up ぐらいですが、文章の中でなら、ほかのものもよく見かけます。

日本語の「笑う」はこの中の「laugh」と対で考えられがちですが、「笑う」の方がはるかに広い範囲をカバーしています。英語の laugh は「ハハハハ！」と軽快に楽しく、声を出して笑う時にだけ使う言葉ですが、日本語では顔が笑みを浮かべている状態はほぼすべて「笑う」で表現することが可能です。

図にするとこんな具合です。

また、ridicule、jeer、mock の三つに注目して考えると、日本語と英語の「笑い」のちがいはもっとはっきり見えてきます。この三つの「笑い方」は日本語では「あざ笑う」というひとつの表現でまかなわれていますが、ridicule は「相手を笑いものにすること」を指し、jeer は「やーい、やーい」と、いじめっ子がするようなあざけ笑いを指し、mock は「相手をこけにするように笑うこと」という風に、本当に微妙な差で三つの言葉は別々の状態を表現しています。

これらのちがいは、日本人には理解するのが極めて難しいものです。そもそも日本人はこの三つを区別していないので、明確にどれかひとつの笑い方を選んで行うことがないからです。何しろこれらすべての単語が、日本語では基本的に「笑う」という一言に

> 1. Crush the graham crackers into crumbs. Mix the soft brown sugar and melted butter into the crackers and mix well. Spread in pie dish. Press mixture with fingers until thin to form the piecrust. Cool in refrigerator.

集約されているわけですから。──図にするとこんな感じになるでしょうか。

ちなみにこの図でそれぞれの英語の円が少しずつ「笑う」の輪からはみ出しているのは、laugh にも jeer にも mock にも ridicule にも、「笑う」にはない意味やニュアンスがちょっとずつ入っているからです。やはりどこまでいっても、円がぴったり重なるということはあり得ません。

世界の区切りが変わる時

さらに分かりやすい例をいくつか見てみましょう。
日本語ではこれをなんと呼んでいますか？

2. Heat oven to 190℃. Beat sugar, melted butter, corn syrup, salt and eggs in medium bowl with hand beater until well blended. Stir in pecans.

では、こっちは？

日本語ではあごに生えている「ひげ」と鼻の下に生えている「ひげ」は同じ「ひげ」ですが、英語で考える人にとっては、あごひげは **beard**、口ひげは **mustache** という異なる二つのものです。その二つを同時に表現する言葉というのは存在しません。大げさに言うと、この二つは英語ではちがう物質として捉えられているのです。

← beard   mustache →

ここまではっきりしたものばかりではありませんが、一見単純な言葉の内側にも、こういう「日本語とのずれ」はいっぱい隠されています。

たとえば、「あまえる」という言葉は英語にはありません。「あまえる」という考え方自体が欧米に存在しないからです。子供が親にあまえている場合にはまだ言い方もありますが、自立心の強い欧米では、大人が大人にあまえるような行為そのものが理解できないからです。当然、それを表現する言葉も必要ありません。だから、日本人が見て「あまえている」と感じる行為でも、欧米人の目にはただ「寄り添っている」とか、悪い意味で「油断させようとしている」といった別の行為に見えてしまいます。

3. Pour into pie plate. Bake 40〜50 minutes or until lightly brown. Cover with foil if crust starts to burn. Serve warm.

Big Fat Cat vs. Mr. Jones

日本人が見ると「あまえている」 　　　欧米人が見ると「寄り添っている」

　さらにもうひとつ別の例です。――日本の色鉛筆のセットにはたいてい「肌色」という、うすいベージュのような色が含まれています。でも、多民族の国では当然「肌の色」が決まっていないので、そんな色鉛筆は存在しません。

　では、日本の「肌色」と同じ色の色鉛筆にはなんという名前がついているのかというと、「**peach**」です。**peach** は果物の「桃」のことですが、確かに桃の内側のうすいベージュ色は日本の「肌色」に近い色をしています。

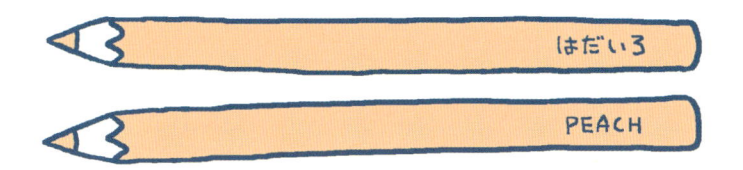

　ところがややこしいことに、「桃色」という色は日本では別の色を指しています。ベージュというよりはピンクに近い色です。そして、この「ピンク」という色は、また別の色として英語に存在しています。

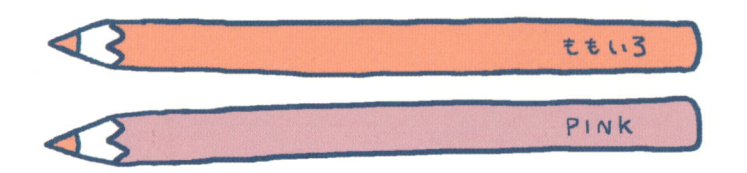

こういうことを考え始めると、普段常識だと考えている枠組みがいかにもろいものかというのが見えてきます。動作の区別も、ものの名前も、色のちがいも、実はそんなに確かなものではないのです。外国語を学ぶ面白さというのは、もしかしたらこういうところにあるのかもしれません。

　人間はどうしても世界に存在する物質や動作や概念を自分の国の言葉の枠組みで区切りがちです。ひとつの言葉で表されるものはひとつのもの——そう考えるのがふつうです。ところが、話す言語が変わってしまうと、その範囲が意外なほど簡単にずれてしまって、常識が覆ってしまいます。

　他国の言葉を学んでいると、そんな驚きに何度もぶつかります。どういうわけかほかの国であっても、単語がちがうだけで区切る枠組みは同じだと人間は思いこみがちです。でも、別の国の言葉を学ぶということは、ただ別のセットの単語表をもらうということではなく、世界のすべての要素を新たに区切り直して考えることです。今まで名前のなかったものに名前がつくこともあります。逆に名前がなくなることもあります。

　外国語を学ぶということは、何も知らなかった子供時代に戻って、もう一度世界の名前をすべて学び直すようなものです。これはまさに未知なる「失われた領域」への冒険の始まりです。

The national #1 best-seller novel!　NOW IN PAPERBACK!
SPYGLASS　by Drake Thurman
A graphic suspense novel set in the woods of the Spyglass County!
BUY IT AT GOLDEN BOOKS in the New Everville Mall

名前のないものたち

　中でも「名前がないものに名前がつく」というのは特に不思議な経験です。特別な輸入品や日本には存在しない製品のことを言っているわけではありません。ごくふつうの日常的な動作や感覚でも、日本語では名前のついていないものが意外なほどたくさんあります。

　reputation という単語を例にとってみましょう。

　reputation は「今までずっとあることをあるやり方でしてきたので、当然今回もそうするであろうと思われていること」という、日本語にすると少し複雑な意味になってしまう単語です。日本語にはこれに相当する日常的な言葉がありません。

　ちょっとジェレミーに実際にこの単語を使ってもらいましょう。

それはやめた方がいいと思うよ。 　　心配するな。おれにはこういうことをするっていう reputation があるんだ。 　　ぐわあああああ！

　ここでの reputation を日本語に入れ替えるとしたら、かろうじてあてはまるのは「評判」や「名声」ぐらいですが、これらはどちらも比較的よいイメージのある言葉なので、英語の reputation とは、受ける印象がだいぶ変わってしまいます。これは一番大切なニュアンスである、「もともと悪いからこれ以上悪くならない評価」という免罪符のような

意味が「失われた領域」に入ってしまっているからです。

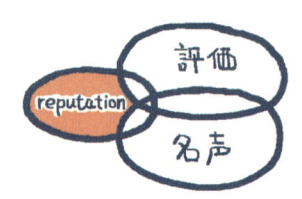

ほかにも「ニュアンス」、「イメージ」、「モチベーション」など日本語にないため、カタカナで輸入された単語はいっぱいあります。「モチベーション」を翻訳してみると「動機」になりますが、それでは「モチベーション」にある「前向きなエネルギーの元となる動機」という強い感覚が伝わりません。これらはきっと英語でこの言葉を知った人たちが、日本語でもその感覚を伝えたくて無理に使い始め、やがてカタカナとして定着していったものなのでしょう。

一方で、日本語を英語に直す時に消えてしまう領域もあります。日本語にはたくさんある「擬音」という要素は英語には少ししかありません。「何かが当たる音」として使う言葉は英語では **slam** か **crash** ぐらいのものですが、日本語には無数に存在します。「バン」「ドカン」「ガン」「ドン」「ポン」などの多彩な「擬音」は、日本語から英語に訳した時点ですべて失われてしまうものです。

日本語ではまったくちがうこれら三つの音も、英語ではひとつになってしまいます。

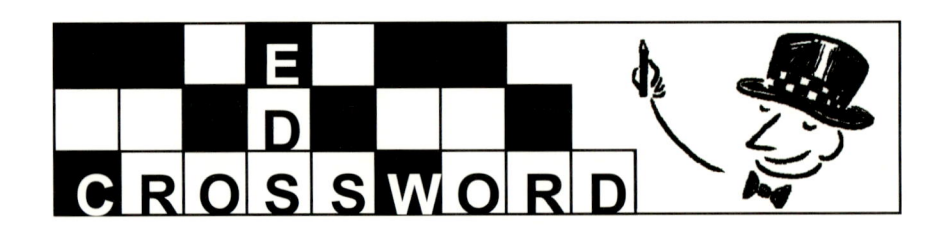

Big Fat Cat vs. Mr. Jones

　一方、英語には強調の言葉がたくさんあります。日本語では「ものすごく」や「めちゃくちゃ」あたりが最高レベルですが、英語ではスラングを含めれば、さらに十段階ぐらい先までの大げさな強調用の言葉が用意されています。このため、英語で「めちゃくちゃすごい」よりもすごいものが出てくると、どんなにすごいものでも、翻訳の時点で全部「めちゃくちゃすごい」というレベルにまで落とされてしまいます。それ以上の激しい感情を表現する言葉が日本語にはないからです。これらも翻訳の途中で「失われた領域」に漂い続ける部分です。

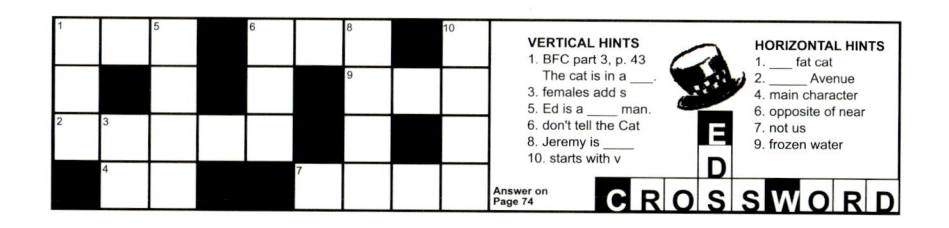

おまえ、すごいよ！
You're great!

おまえ、本当にすごいよ！
You're really great!

おまえ、めちゃくちゃすごいよ！
You're incredible!

（同等の表現なし）
You're amazing!

（同等の表現なし）
You're unbelievable!

（同等の表現なし）
You're goddamn great!

（同等の表現なし）
You're（放送禁止のため掲載不可）！

VERTICAL HINTS
1. BFC part 3, p. 43 The cat is in a ___.
3. females add s
5. Ed is a ___ man.
6. don't tell the Cat
8. Jeremy is ___
10. starts with v

HORIZONTAL HINTS
1. ___ fat cat
2. ___ Avenue
4. main character
6. opposite of near
7. not us
9. frozen water

Answer on Page 74

CROSSWORD

「意味」の裏にある「イメージ」

この「失われた領域」にあるものは得てして重要な意味合いを持っているにも関わらず、辞書に載せることも、学校で教えることもできません。なぜなら、その部分は時代や場所によって、どんどん変動する曖昧な部分だからです。自分で感じ取っていく以外に理解する方法がない部分——その単語の持つ「イメージ」の部分だからです。

普段はあまり意識しませんが、すべての単語には「意味」のほかに「イメージ」があります。辞書には「意味」の方しか載っていませんが、単語にとって「イメージ」というのはとても大切なものです。その言葉はどんなタイプの人が、どういう時に、どんな感情から、誰に向かって使い、どんな効果を期待するものか……この要素だけはどうしても翻訳の過程で失われてしまいます。単語レベルでもそうですから、文章ともなるとなおさらです。たとえばこんな文章で見てみましょう。

She is expecting a baby.

expect の意味はほとんどの辞書では「期待する」と書かれています。この文章をそのまま訳すと、「彼女は赤ちゃんを期待している」となります。

意味の上ではこれで合っています。ただ、やはり失われてしまったものがあります。

それは期待する意思の「強さ」です。

日本文の方は、漠然と赤ちゃんが欲しいと思っているだけです。しかし、英文の方で

は、この女性はおそらくすでに妊娠していて、近い将来出産することが分かっている上で、それを expect しています。

「期待する」　　　　　　　「expect」

expect という単語にはただ「期待する」という意味だけではなく、「当然くるであろうものを期待する」という、より強いイメージがあります。「expect」と「期待する」のちがいはその部分にあるのですが、残念ながら翻訳を読んでいても、その感覚は伝わってきません。

「期待」する範囲がより大きい expect

「イメージ」がもたらす影響は時として「意味」以上に大きなものです。ひとつの単語を本当に覚えるということは、その単語が持っている意味をただ暗記することではなく、その単語のイメージが頭の中で完成するまで、何度も何度もちがうシチュエーションでその単語と出会い、印象づけられることです。このシリーズで、とにかく英語の本──特に物語──を読んでほしいと繰り返し言ってきたのも、それが大きな理由です。

"TRUST OUR CRUST!"
STATE PIE FESTIVAL
HELD AT THE NEW EVERVILLE MALL DEC.15-24 A.M.9:00-P.M.7:00

自分だけの言語

　「意味」だけで「イメージ」を持たない単語は決して有効に使うことができません。心に残っている「イメージ」のある単語だけが自分にとっての本当の言葉です。
　laugh という単語を覚える時、それを単純に「**laugh** ＝笑う」と暗記してしまうと、**laugh** の持っている「軽い、軽快な笑い」のイメージも「失われた領域」へ消えてしまいます。その方法で覚えた **laugh** は英米人が使っている **laugh** と比べて、とても薄っぺらな言葉になっています。**laugh** という単語を覚えるときに本当に必要なのは、誰かの笑う姿です。「笑う」という日本語が頭の中に出てきても、それは **laugh** ではありません。「**laugh** しているイメージ」が浮かんだ時にはじめて、英語を母国語として話している人たちの感覚がつかめたことになります。

The cat scratched Ed.

　ここまで **BFC** シリーズを読んできてくださったみなさんなら、この一文を見て、頭の中にある絵が浮かんだのではないでしょうか？　もし浮かんだなら、それはこれらの単語を本当に覚えたということになります。もう、これらの単語が頭ではなく、心に入っているということです。それはもう「意味」ではありません。「イメージ」です。
　覚えようと意識して読む必要はありません。楽しんで読むだけで十分です。イメージを作るのは、心が勝手にやってくれます。口から入れた食べ物が、意識しなくても体内で栄養に変わるように、知識も必要なものだけを身体が選んで吸収してくれます。
　英語と日本語は似ているようでも、たくさんのちがいがあります。だから「英語の学習＝英語を日本語に変換する」というのはあまりにもったいない考え方です。翻訳するなら、「**cry** ＝泣く」のような言葉の置き換えではなく、

Making a great city greater!
JOIN THE FOR-EVERVILLE PROJECT
for more information, contact the Everville City Hall

Big Fat Cat vs. Mr. Jones

cry =

というように、自分が決して忘れられないイメージに交換してみてください。そのためにエドや、猫や、ジェレミーや、ウィリーがいます。世界中のすべての物語のキャラクターは、そのために本の世界で読者がくるのを待っています。

辞書の正しい使い方

とはいっても、「イメージ」が最初にできあがるまでは、その単語を理解するための手がかりとして、日本語に翻訳してみるのもひとつの手です。でも、そこで止まってしまってはいけません。日本語に訳すだけでは、どうしても「失われた領域」ができてしまいます。

その「失われた領域」を自分で埋めていくための便利な道具が辞書です。ただ、辞書は使い方がよく誤解されている道具でもあります。

辞書の中ではたいていひとつの単語に対して、複数の意味が載せられています。辞書を引いて、もし三つの意味が書いてあれば、多くの人は適しているものを、そのうちのどれかから選ぼうとします。しかし、辞書にたくさんの意味が載っているのは、本当は「この中から選んでください」ということではなく、三つの意味が載っているなら、三つ

Jeremy Lightfoot Jr.'s
Words of Wisdom

"The three important things in life: Love, money, and the love of money."

Jeremy Lightfoot Jr.

全部でその単語の意味ということです。

　試しに **run** という単語を英和辞典で引いてみましょう。いくつもの意味がこんな形で載っています。

run fast　　　run a machine　　　run a company　　　run for president

走る　　　　　運転する　　　　　経営する　　　　　　立候補する

run という単語の総合的なイメージ

ちがう文化ではひとつで表せる単語が、日本語では複数でないと表せないために意味

を並べているわけです。辞書を引く側はその複数の単語から、左ページの図のような要領で「だいたい総合的には、こういうイメージなのかな」と漠然とあたりをつけて、また英語の世界へ戻っていくことになります。──これが本来の英和辞典の使い方です。

　でも、できるならその前に、前後関係やストーリー、キャラクターの性格や物語の展開から、その分からない単語の意味を想像してみてください。そうすれば、イメージはもっと頭に入りやすくなります。その上で辞書を引くのはとても効果的です。

　本を読む時の辞書の引き方にもちょっとしたコツがあります。よかったら参考にしてください。

（**1**）一回目は多少無理をしてでも辞書を使わず（どうしても必要なら最小限だけ引いて）、二回目に読むときに分からなかった単語を引いていく。

（**2**）あらかじめ数ページの間の分からない単語を辞書で引き、ルビを振っておいた上で、辞書を伏せて読む。

（**3**）翻訳があるものなら先にそれを読み、ストーリーを頭に入れてから、もう一度英語で読む。

　どの方法でもかまいませんが、できれば（**1**）の方法をおすすめします。もし（**1**）の方法で意味が分からない単語がたくさん見つかってしまったなら、思い切ってその本は後回しにして、もう少し難易度の低いものに挑戦してみてください。最初は難易度をとことん落としてみるのもいいことです。

　無理して映画の原作を読むより、気軽に絵本を読んでみてください。「今さら絵本なんて」と思うかもしれませんが、世界中で絵本を子供だけのものだと思っているのは日本

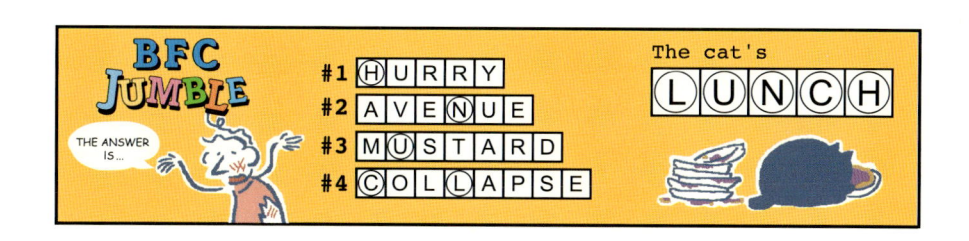

人ぐらいです。英語の絵本には大人が読んでも面白いものがたくさんあります。試しに何冊か読んでみて、本当に絵本が子供だけのものかどうか、ぜひ自分で判断してみてください。

　英語の学び方は無数にあります。正しい方法も、間違った方法もありません。自分になじむものがあれば、ためらわずやってみてください。どんな学び方であれ、楽しむことができればそれが一番です。英語が好きになれたら、それでいいんです。

余裕があるから言葉になれる

　翻訳で失われてしまうもの──それを追いかけてここまで来ましたが、それは時に話し手の「個性」や「気持ち」であったり、「価値観」であったり、また「国民性」「習慣」「考え方」であったりします。「楽しさ」や「やさしさ」が失われてしまうこともよくあります。

　でも、もっとずっと簡単で分かりやすい言葉で、これらの「失われたもの」をすべて表現できます。

　失われているのは、話し手の「心」です。

　言葉がイメージを持っている限り、その言葉を選んだ話し手の思いがこもっているのは当然です。その人は、その言葉でなければならなかったから、その言葉を選んだはずです。どんなに近い代用品であっても、代わりのものでは、その気持ちを表すことはできません。

　英語は生きています。今、こうしている間にも世界のどこかで誰かが使っている言葉です。そして、その人たちは辞書のように考えたり、ルールに従って動いたりはしていません。文の途中で気持ちが変わることもあれば、単語の意味を勘違いしていることも

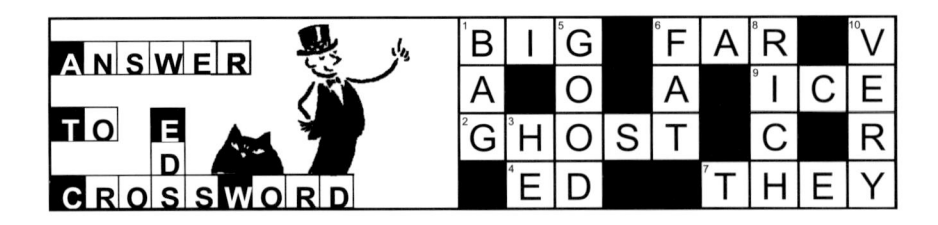

あり、独自の言葉を発明したりすることさえあります。そのため、英語を理解するのに辞書やルールに頼るばかりでは限界があって当然です。

　「英語」自体を理解するのは簡単です。でも、人間を理解するのは、それが日本人であっても、アメリカ人であっても、難しいことです。ましてやそれが慣れていない言語を通してならなおさらです。

　外国語が分からないのは多くの場合、言語能力や理解力が足りないからではなく、人間同士のコミュニケーションがもともと難しいからです。その上で育った文化や環境がちがうのですから、無理もないことです。外国語が間に入っているので、それが原因のように思えますが、日本人と日本語で話していても、相手の真意というのはどれほど感じ取れているものなのでしょうか？　言語の壁がないので、「言葉」を言い訳にできないだけで、その代わり「年齢」や「性別」、「個性」や「地位」が言い訳になるだけではないでしょうか。

　英語は日本人を苦しめるためのものではありません。むしろ英語は文化も世界観もちがう人々を理解するための貴重な架け橋です。

　言葉は曖昧にできています。つかむのが難しいぼんやりとしたものです。でも、だからこそ人の心を伝える道具になれます。そんな曖昧なものを正確に変換したり、さらにそれに点数をつけたりすることなんてできるはずがありません。少しぐらい分かりにくいところがあっても、英語が英語のままでいることを許してあげてください。言葉が動き回れるだけの余裕を残しておいてあげてください。そうすれば言葉は心の中で成長し、進化し、広がります。

　余裕があるからこそ言葉は言葉になり得ます。その余裕を「失われた領域」にしてしまうか、「人間らしさ」にするかは、いつだって使う人次第です。

MOOCHIES
The end of the world has landed next door!
Welcome, Monsieur!

TIPS FROM THE CAT:
言い回しの種明かし

英語の物語を読んでいく上での、
BFCからのちょっとしたヒント集。
今回は本編にひそんでいる「言い回し」の数々
——種明かしをどうぞ。

『ビッグ・ファット・キャット vs ミスター・ジョーンズ』、楽しんでいただけましたでしょうか？　ついにシリーズも五巻目となり、エドと猫の冒険もクライマックスが近づいてきました。

　ところでお気づきになりましたか？　今回は本編に何カ所か※印がふってあるものがあります。この印の付いたフレーズは、どれも前回の解説で登場した「言い回し」の一種です。知っているととても面白い表現なのですが、そうでなければ、いくら考えても意味の分からないものばかりです。

　BFC BOOKS では読みやすさを考えて、可能な限りこういう表現を避けてきたのですが、言い回しも英語の面白さの一部なので、今回からは少しだけ忍び込ませてあります。とはいえ物語の展開上重要なところにはありませんので、一回目はとばしてもらって、二回目で読んでもらってもかまいません。もし余裕があればクイズのような気分で、どんな意味か想像してみて、そのあとでこのページを読んでみるのも面白いかもしれません。

　それでは今回登場した言い回しの種明かしです。

the time draws near（p.15）
draw は相当広い範囲をカバーしている、日本語にはない矢印です。訳語として最初に浮かぶのは「描く」かもしれませんが、もともとは「引く」ことを指しています。描くことを **draw** というのは、「線を引く」から進化したものです。ここで近くに引っぱっているのは「**time**」です。未来の締め切り時間が少しずつ現在の方へ近づいてくる感じで、タイムリミットが近づいてくる緊迫感を出しています。ちなみに **pull** とのちがいは、くじ引きのように、「引く」という言葉の中に「引いて選ぶ」というニュアンスが含まれているところにあります。

a trick of the eye（p.16）
そのまま「目のトリック」です。自分の目が自分に対していたずら（トリック）を仕掛

TIPS FROM THE CAT:
言い回しの種明かし

英語の物語を読んでいく上での、
BFC からのちょっとしたヒント集。
今回は本編にひそんでいる「言い回し」の数々
──種明かしをどうぞ。

『ビッグ・ファット・キャット vs ミスター・ジョーンズ』、楽しんでいただけましたでしょうか？　ついにシリーズも五巻目となり、エドと猫の冒険もクライマックスが近づいてきました。

　ところでお気づきになりましたか？　今回は本編に何カ所か※印がふってあるものがあります。この印の付いたフレーズは、どれも前回の解説で登場した「言い回し」の一種です。知っているととても面白い表現なのですが、そうでなければ、いくら考えても意味の分からないものばかりです。

　BFC BOOKS では読みやすさを考えて、可能な限りこういう表現を避けてきたのですが、言い回しも英語の面白さの一部なので、今回からは少しだけ忍び込ませてあります。とはいえ物語の展開上重要なところにはありませんので、一回目はとばしてもらって、二回目で読んでもらってもかまいません。もし余裕があればクイズのような気分で、どんな意味か想像してみて、そのあとでこのページを読んでみるのも面白いかもしれません。

　それでは今回登場した言い回しの種明かしです。

the time draws near（p.15）
draw は相当広い範囲をカバーしている、日本語にはない矢印です。訳語として最初に浮かぶのは「描く」かもしれませんが、もともとは「引く」ことを指しています。描くことを **draw** というのは、「線を引く」から進化したものです。ここで近くに引っぱっているのは「**time**」です。未来の締め切り時間が少しずつ現在の方へ近づいてくる感じで、タイムリミットが近づいてくる緊迫感を出しています。ちなみに **pull** とのちがいは、くじ引きのように、「引く」という言葉の中に「引いて選ぶ」というニュアンスが含まれているところにあります。

a trick of the eye（p.16）
そのまま「目のトリック」です。自分の目が自分に対していたずら（トリック）を仕掛

けている、転じて「目の錯覚」という意味になります。

going crazy（p.22）

crazy は一般的に「狂っている状態」を指します。狂気へ **go** するというとあまりいい意味合いではないように聞こえますが、**crazy** には少しユーモラスで、「狂ってるけどいかしてる」という肯定的な要素が含まれています。ここでは狂ったように騒ぐ観客の盛り上がりを、アナウンサーがこう表現しています。

sort of rings a bell（p.27）

何かを「思いついた」「思い出した」時には、日本の漫画ではよく頭の上で電球が点くという表現が用いられますが、英語の文章でも同じことが「鐘を鳴らす」という表現で出てきます。**sort of** は日本語の「なんとなく」にあたる言葉です。

Holy cow / Holy macaroni（p.27 / p.29）

深い意味はまったくありません。アメリカでは **Holy**（「聖なる」）にもっともふさわしくない単語をくっつけてよく驚きを表現します。マカロニや牛（**cow**）は語呂もいいので定番化しています。ほかにも **Holy cat** などいろいろなパターンがあります。

all for the best（p.37）

日本語で近いフレーズは「終わりよければすべてよし」です。「いいことも悪いことも含めて、何もかもが最後にはよい方向に行った」という意味のよく耳にする言い回しです。もう少し弱い言い方では、**all for the better** というのもあります。

　言い回しはことわざのようなもので、日常の会話の中のちょっとしたスパイスです。知っていると確かに便利ですが、あまり頼りすぎると、ことわざや四字熟語を連発してしゃべっているような奇妙な印象を受けてしまいます。だから、言い回しをリストにして覚えるようなことはせず、物語や会話の中に出てきたものに自然と触れていってください。そうすれば、どの言い回しが、どんな人に、どのくらいの頻度で使われているのかも同時に知ることができます。

BFC SPECIAL FEATURE:

A NIGHT AT THE CINEMA

Script by Takahiko Mukoyama
Breakdowns by Yoji Takemura
Art by Tetsuo Takashima

THE WORLD IS A COLD PLACE.
YOU'VE LEARNED THAT IN YOUR TWELVE YEARS HERE.
LIVING MEANS PAIN.
BUT DEATH ALSO MEANS PAIN. SO THE WORLD IS BASICALLY FILLED WITH PAIN.
THAT SMELL.
ALWAYS FROM THIS BUILDING.
A SWEET SMELL.
NO MORE PAIN. ENOUGH PAIN.
NOW PLAYING
NO MORE TAKING.
NOW, THE GIVING.
DON'T MOVE!

Panel 1: "YOUR WALLET! GIVE ME YOUR WALLET!"

THE SWEET SMELL IS EVERYWHERE.

Panel 2: "I DON'T HAVE ONE."

"SHUT UP! JUST GIVE ME YOUR WALLET!"

Panel 3: "I SAID I DON'T HAVE ONE."

"HERE, THIS IS ALL I HAVE."

THE PLAN. IT'S NOT WORKING.

Panel 4: THINK.

DON'T PANIC.

DON'T PANIC.

Panel 5: "FUCK YOU!"

BLAM

Panel 6: "SEE! IT'S A REAL GUN. I CAN KILL YOU. I CAN FUCKIN' KILL YOU!!"

DON'T PANIC.

WHY ISN'T HE SCARED?
WHY AM I SCARED?
WHAT'S WRONG?
THINK!
YOU SHOULD BE CAREFUL WITH THAT HAND, KID.
SOME OF THAT GLASS GOT YOU.
GLASS?
OH SHIT!
PAIN.
MORE PAIN.
HERE, LET ME SEE.
DON'T COME NEAR ME!

WHY ISN'T HE SCARED?
THE SWEET SMELL.
ALL AROUND.
SHOOT, NOW!
HE'LL CALL THE COPS!
SHOOT...
LET'S TAKE A LOOK AT THAT WOUND.
THE WHITE MAN FIXES MY HAND.
I TRY TO FOCUS ON THE SMELL.
THE SMELL IS GOOD.
IT SMELLS LIKE MOTHER.
TOO BAD I DON'T HAVE ONE.

THERE. WHAT'S YOUR NAME, KID?
YOU DO HAVE A NAME, DON'T YOU?
BB
SMELL. JUST FOCUS ON THE SMELL.
WELL, BB. YOU SURE CHOSE A BAD TIME AND PLACE TO ROB.
THIS OLD CINEMA, IT'S ALMOST OUT OF MONEY.
THEY HAVEN'T PAID ME FOR TWO MONTHS NOW.
WHY THE HELL DID YOU CHOOSE A CINEMA TO BUST?
YOU DO KNOW WHAT A CINEMA IS?
FOCUS.
IT SMELLED GOOD.

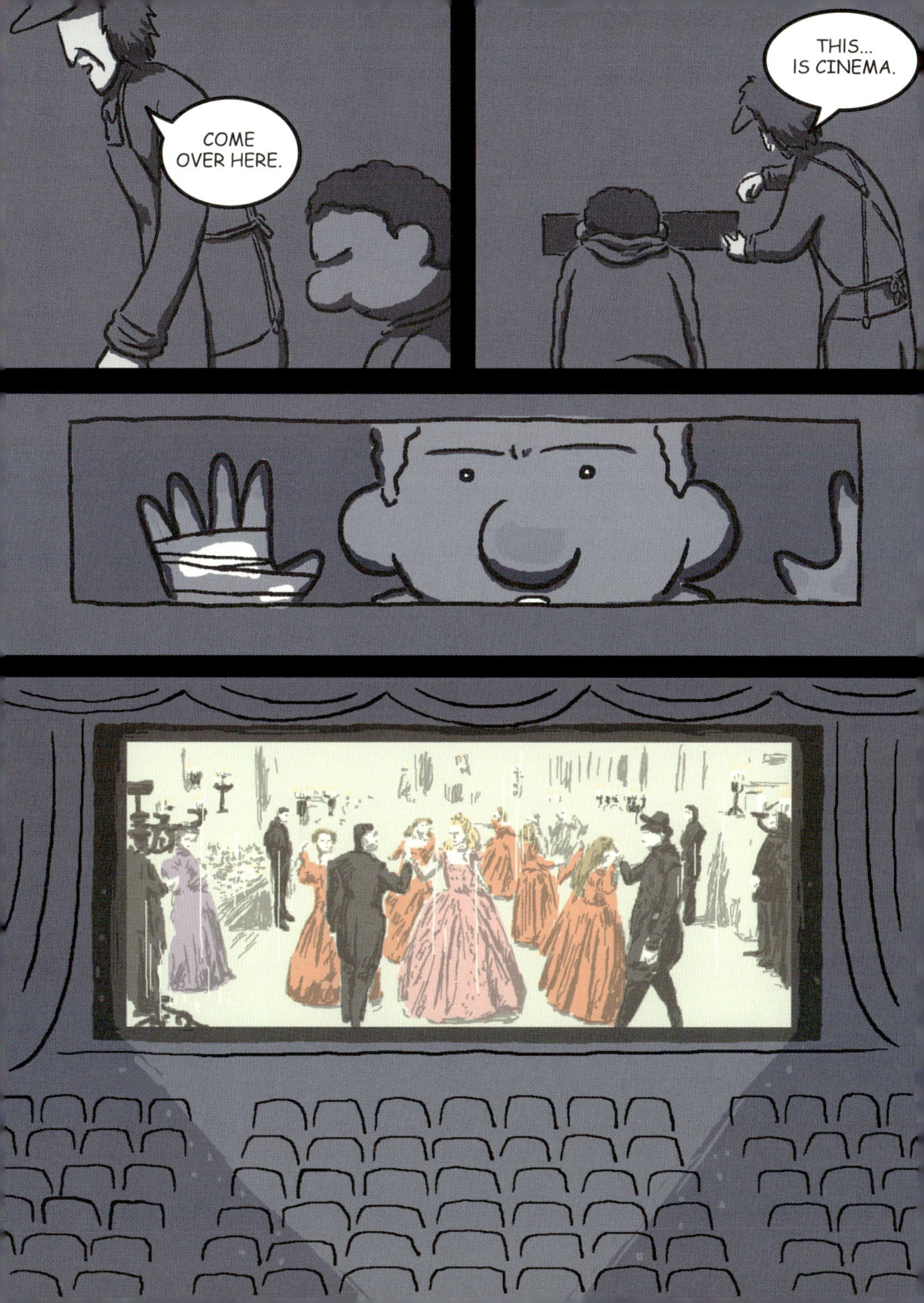
COME OVER HERE.
THIS... IS CINEMA.

POPCORN?
THE SMELL.
THE SWEET SMELL.
IT ALSO TASTES SWEET.
NOW PLAYING
LOOK, KID. I KNOW YOU HAVE TO LIVE. BUT GO EASY ON THE GUN, OKAY?
SOMETIMES IT DOES HIT.
HERE'S A SOUVENIR FOR YOU.
THE WORLD IS A COLD PLACE.
WELL... MOST OF IT ANYWAY.

SOME ARE LUCKY.
THEY LIVE IN WARM PLACES.
I'M NOT ONE OF THEM.
TOO BAD.
SO I HAVE TO LIVE WITH THE PAIN.
TOO BAD.
I WILL LEARN TO DEAL WITH IT.
I WILL LEARN TO CONTROL IT.
I WILL LIVE THIS LIFE...
...THE BEST I CAN.
The End

A NIGHT AT THE CINEMA

—解説—

　一口に英語といっても、たくさんの種類があります。BFC シリーズ本編はとてもオーソドックスなスタイルのナレーションを使っていますが、ほかのスタイルのものに触れてみるのも楽しいものです。今回収録した短編、「A Night at the Cinema」はコミックのスタイルに、かなり言葉少ない独白のナレーションがついています。ハードボイルド小説などでも見受けられる文体で、少し難易度の高い形です。雰囲気を重視してあえてルビをつけていませんので、戸惑った方も多いと思います。分かりにくいと感じた場合は、物語中に登場する文章に、大きく分けて三つの種類があることを頭に入れておくと読みやすくなります。

1. 声に出して言っている通常のセリフ（丸いフキダシで囲まれている文字）
2. 主人公がナレーターとなって、自分の人生を客観的に語る文章
　（You で自分自身に語りかける形。82 ページ 1 コマ目の文章など）
3. その場での主人公の考えを、そのまま短い言葉で表現している文章
　（82 ページ 3 コマ目の文章など）

　また、全体を通してよく出てくる二つのキーワードに注目してみると、流れをつかみやすくなるかもしれません。

pain: 肉体的なもの、精神的なもの、すべてをひっくるめた「痛み」。
smell: 映画館に漂う、できたてのポップコーンの香り。甘い香りであることから、おそらくはキャラメルポップコーン。極めて貧しい主人公の少年は香りの正体を知らない。

　このタイプの物語は言葉の数を最小限に抑えて書かれているため、何度も読み返して、消えている部分を少しずつ想像で補うことが前提となっています。英語はそもそも日本語よりも中性的で、話し手の感情が出にくい言語です。そのため、物語の中の激しい出来事の裏に、奇妙に冷静なナレーションをつけることで、独特の静かな雰囲気が発生します。この形のナレーションは日本語ではなかなか再現できないため、この機会に英語ならではのリズム感を楽しんでいただけたらと考えて収録しました。
　英語の別の側面からの面白さを感じてもらえたならうれしい限りです。しかし、好みの分かれる文章と内容のため、ぴんとこなくても、あまり気にしないでください。いろんな英語があるという感覚だけでも感じてもらえれば十分です。

BFC EXTRA SPECIAL
パイ・コンテスト・フライヤー

パイ・フェスティバルがエヴァーヴィルにやってくる！
パイの大好きな人も、そうでない人も、
みんなニュー・モールへ集合！

STATE PIE CONTEST

AT
NEW EVERVILLE MALL
DEC. 24th

GOLDEN CRUST
CHAMPIONSHIP

STATE PIE

3:00 P.M. — ALL NATURAL NO PRESERVATIVES

Welcome, folks, to the annual State Pie Festival! competing for the ultimate dream award for all pie you can purchase and take home your favorite pie PIEGAMES is sponsored by the New Everville Mall

Brown Butters — since 1961 —

LUCKY TREE — APPLE PIE

Cake In A Bag! — Doggie Bag

Buffi Brothers — 100% PURE VIRGIN OLIVE OIL

SMACKY #1

GOO GOO PLANET — NOT FROM YOUR PLANET!

SUGAR & SPICE — Serving Excellent Chinese Cuisine To The Spyglass County For Twenty Five Years

FRUIT IN A CRUST — The only real fruit pie in the state

CONTEST

This year, we have eighteen unique pie shops bakers — The Golden Crust! After the match, and decide for yourself, the best pie of all! The and the Spyglass County. **Enjoy your slice!**

ALEXANDER'S DRUG STORES

EAT OUR PIE AT CAFES INSIDE STORE

TIC TAC TOE

Make a Donation
Contact us 0210-050-XXXX

FROZEN DOZEN

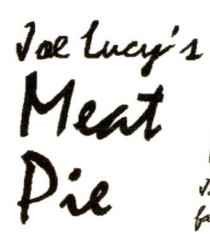

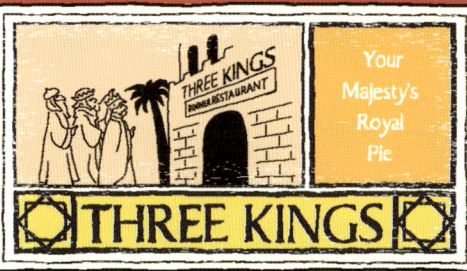

16 FLAVORS, 25 VARIATIONS, 16 SYRUPS

MOTHER ANN KETCHUM

Joe Lucy's Meat Pie

Jane (my granddaughter)'s favorite recipe!

THREE KINGS

THREE KINGS DINNER RESTAURANT

Your Majesty's Royal Pie

ZOMBIE PIES

ADULTS HATE US BUT THEIR KIDS SURE LOVE US!

Good Kid's Treat

Have you behaved yourself today?

Ed's MAGIC PIE SHOP

『ビッグ・ファット・キャット vs ミスター・ジョーンズ』の最後に

　BFC BOOKSもついに五冊目を迎えて、今までよりも一歩踏み込んだ内容となりました。今回の「BFC BOOKS PRESENTS」のページでは、ルールやコツといった基本的なしくみを超えて、言葉の本質的な不思議さと曖昧さに触れています。「A → B」と機械的に読むことに慣れすぎてほしくないからです。

　確かに言葉にはある程度のルールや規則性があります。その部分は採点したり、善し悪しを決めることも可能です。でも、なぜか分からないけれど心を打つ言葉、生涯忘れられない一言、相手を好きにさせるセリフ、嫌いにさせるセリフ……というような、どんなルールでも説明のつかない不思議な力も言葉は秘めています。それはルールの正しさとはなんの関係もありません。それどころか、もっとも感動的な言葉は得てして文法がでたらめなものであったりします。

　最初はみんな言葉のそんな不思議な部分に憧れて学びはじめます。しかし、残念ながらルールの渦に巻き込まれるうち、いつしかそんな力が言葉にあることさえ忘れてしまいます。ルールですべてが説明できて、そういう不思議な感覚はただの錯覚であったかのように思えてきます。でも、言葉には確かに説明のできない不思議な力があります。

　学生時代に「英語」という教科にこてんぱんにされて、今でも英語に苦手意識のある方は、ぜひ言葉のそういった側面をもう一度探してみてください。最初に外国語の存在を知った時に感じた、あの不思議な感覚がきっとよみがえってきます。もう一度「自分の言葉は通じる」と、心から信じられるようになります。

　ふつうの英語、変わった英語、難しい英語、へんてこりんな英語、言葉少ない英語、壊れた英語、いやな英語、見たこともない英語……

　全部、英語です。教科書に載っている英語はそのうちのひとつに過ぎません。「正しい英語」ではないんです。だから、自分の英語は自分だけの英語だと自信を持って使ってください。

　そうすれば、言葉はきっと不思議な力を発揮し始めます。

　　　　　　Good luck, happy readings, and see you again at the pie festival!
　　　　　　　　　　　　　　　　　　　　　　　　　　　　　向山貴彦

　　当シリーズは英文法の教科書ではなく、あくまで「英語を読む」ことを最大の目的として作られています。そのため、従来の英文法とはいささか異なる解釈を用いている部分があります。これらの相違は英語に取り組み始めたばかりの方にも親しみやすくするため、あえて取り入れたものです。

STAFF

written and produced by Takahiko Mukoyama	企画・原作・文・解説 向山貴彦
illustrated by Tetsuo Takashima	絵・キャラクターデザイン たかしまてつを
rewritten by Tomoko Yoshimi	文章校正 吉見知子
art direction by Yoji Takemura	アートディレクター 竹村洋司
DTP by Aya Nakamura	DTP 中村文
technical advice by Takako Inoue	テクニカルアドバイザー 井上貴子
edited by Masayasu Ishihara Shoji Nagashima Atsushi Hino	編集 石原正康（幻冬舎） 永島賞二（幻冬舎） 日野淳（幻冬舎）
editorial assistance by Yutaka Inoue Daisaku Takeda Kaori Miyayama	編集協力 井上裕 武田大作 宮山香里
English-language editing by Michael Keezing	英文校正 マイクル・キージング（keezing.communications）
supportive design by Akira Hirakawa Miyuki Matsuda	デザイン協力 平川彰（幻冬舎デザイン室） 松田美由紀（幻冬舎デザイン室）
supervised by Atsuko Mukoyama Yoshihiko Mukoyama	監修 向山淳子（梅光学院大学） 向山義彦（梅光学院大学）
a studio ET CETERA production	製作 スタジオ・エトセトラ
published by GENTOSHA	発行 幻冬舎

special thanks to:

Mac & Jessie Gorham	マック＆ジェシー・ゴーハム
Baiko Gakuin University	梅光学院大学

series dedicated to "Fuwa-chan," our one and only special cat

---

BIG FAT CAT オフィシャルウェブサイト
http://www.studioetcetera.com/bigfatcat

幻冬舎ホームページ
http://www.gentosha.co.jp

〈著者紹介〉
向山貴彦　1970年アメリカ・テキサス州生まれ。作家。製作集団スタジオ・エトセトラを創設。デビュー作『童話物語』(幻冬舎文庫)は、ハイ・ファンタジーの傑作として各紙誌から絶賛された。向山淳子氏、たかしまてつを氏との共著『ビッグ・ファット・キャットの世界一簡単な英語の本』は、英語修得のニュー・スタンダードとして注目を浴び、ミリオンセラーとなった。

たかしまてつを　1967年愛知県生まれ。フリーイラストレーターとして、雑誌等で活躍。1999年イタリアのボローニャ国際絵本原画展入選。著書に『ビッグ・ファット・キャットのグリーティング・カード』(幻冬舎文庫)。

ビッグ・ファット・キャットVSミスター・ジョーンズ
2004年4月10日　第1刷発行
2019年1月31日　第3刷発行

著　者　向山貴彦　たかしまてつを
発行者　見城　徹

発行所　株式会社 幻冬舎
　　　　〒151-0051 東京都渋谷区千駄ヶ谷4-9-7

電話：03(5411)6211(編集)
　　　03(5411)6222(営業)
振替：00120-8-767643
印刷・製本所：株式会社 光邦

検印廃止

万一、落丁乱丁のある場合は送料当社負担でお取替致します。小社宛にお送り下さい。本書の一部あるいは全部を無断で複写複製することは、法律で認められた場合を除き、著作権の侵害となります。定価はカバーに表示してあります。

©TAKAHIKO MUKOYAMA, TETSUO TAKASHIMA, GENTOSHA 2004
Printed in Japan
ISBN 4-344-00496-5 C0095
幻冬舎ホームページアドレス　http://www.gentosha.co.jp/

この本に関するご意見・ご感想をメールでお寄せいただく場合は、
comment@gentosha.co.jpまで。

GENTOSHA

ビッグ・ファット・キャットの三色辞典
～ vs ミスター・ジョーンズ編～

三色辞典の使い方

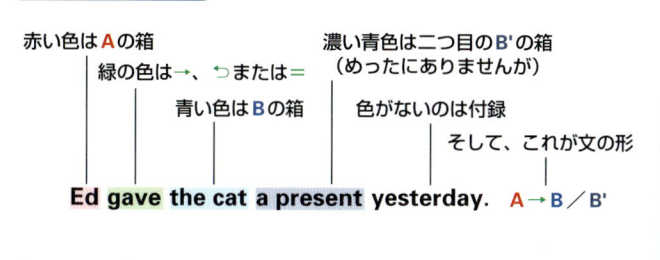

赤い色は **A** の箱
緑の色は →、↻ または ＝
青い色は **B** の箱
濃い青色は二つ目の **B'** の箱
（めったにありませんが）
色がないのは付録
そして、これが文の形

Ed gave the cat a present yesterday.　A→B／B'

分かりにくい文については、ページの右側に少し詳しい解説が載っています。同じ数字のついた文と照らし合わせてご覧ください。

この三色辞典は『ビッグ・ファット・キャットの世界一簡単な英語の本』で紹介されている方法論に基づき、本編の英文を色分けして、解説を加えたヒントブックです。もちろん「答え」ではありません。考える上でのひとつのガイドラインとしてお使いください。

p.52

Ed still hadn't recovered control, but he said to George in a trembling voice.　A→B, but A↩

167. "Heat... two more cups of blueberry in a saucepan."　(A)→B
"Gotcha!"　不完全な文
168. George dashed away, confident that Ed knew a way to repair the pie.　A↩
169. But he didn't.　A↩
He had started scraping the filling out of the crust, but he knew it was impossible.　A→B, but A→B
There was no way to make a pie in seven minutes.　A＝B

167. you が省略されている命令の文です。

168. confident 以下は George の化粧文。ここでの way は「（修理する）道」＝「方法」。

169. 本来は But he didn't.。前文の内容を受けて、「そうではなかった」と否定しています。たった7分でパイを完成させる方法などあるはずがないからです。

160. "... other pie," Ed said again to George, but most of it was drowned out by the sound of the audience.
A→B, but A＝B
"Say what?" George asked close to Ed's ear. A→B
161. "Get the other pie out of the oven! Fast!" Ed repeated, much louder this time. A→B

160. it は直前のかき消されたエドのセリフの代役。

161. エドにしてはかなり乱暴な口調の命令の文。あまりに絶体絶命の状況に、エドも余裕がありません。

p.50

162. Hearing the urgency in Ed's voice, George flew over to the oven and returned quickly with the other pie.
A↺ and (A) ↺
Ed cut this one in half too, and tasted a piece of it.
A→B, and (A) →B
His reaction was almost the same. A＝B
But this time, his face lost color completely. A→B
George also took a piece of the pie and bit into it.
A→B, and (A) →B
Almost instantly, he spit it out. A→B
"God! 不完全な文
What the hell...?" 不完全な文
George turned to Ed. A↺

162. flew という矢印はまさに飛ぶような勢いの移動。run や dash よりさらに速度感があります。

p.51

163. "Someone did something to my stuff," Ed said. A→B
George couldn't understand what Ed said for a moment.
A→B

163. エドには誰かが何かをしたことしか分かりません。stuff も曖昧な言葉なので、すごくぼんやりした文になっています。

164. Then, the full horror sank in. A↺
The pies were ruined. A＝B
There was no more time left. A＝B
Ed glanced at the clock tower. A→B
Seven minutes. 不完全な文

164. この瞬間までは、何が起こっているのかジョージは気がついていなかったのですが、その恐怖がじわっと体に染みこんでくる様子を sank という単語で表現しています。

165. The contest was in full swing. A＝B
Most of the contestants were carrying finished pies from their booths to the judges' area. A＝B
166. Ed could do nothing except stare at the two ruined pies on the table. A→B

165. full swing ─ つまり「振り」が最大になった瞬間。盛り上がりの絶頂です。野球のバッターが全力で打つ時におなじみの表現です。

"Ed!" 不完全な文
George tugged on Ed's sleeve. A→B
"C'mon, Ed! A↺
We still have time! A→B
I'll run and get anything! A↺ and (A) →B
Just tell me what you need!" (A) →B／B'

166. もはやエドにできることといったら except 以下の行動ぐらいです。

p.52

p.48

He was so scared.　A = B
"Hurry, Ed!"　BeeJees said.　A → B
It sounded like a prayer.　A ↩
"Please hurry... Please..."　(A) ↩

p.49

"George!　不完全な文
The oven!　不完全な文
Check the pies!"　(A) → B
George looked towards the back door.　A → B
He saw Ed come running back with a hint of panic in his eyes.　A → B = B'

154. The pies would be done in maybe another five minutes.　A = B
He couldn't understand why Ed was in such a rush.　A → B
"Hey, man.　不完全な文
155. Take it easy.　(A) → B
Everything's fine, man."　A = B
Ed ran past George, grabbed the mitten hanging on the side of the oven, and without any hesitation, opened the oven door.　A ↩, (A) → B, and (A) → B
156. A cloud of smoke rose out of the small door, making Ed and George cough.　A ↩
157. Ed knew immediately that something was terribly wrong.　A → B
There shouldn't be this much smoke inside the oven.　A = B
158. He gulped as the smoke began to clear.　A ↩
As soon as he could see inside, Ed pulled a slightly burned pie out of the oven and hurried over to the table.　A → B and (A) ↩

154.「パイが done になる」とは「パイが焼き上がる」こと。another は実は an と other がくっついた言葉です。another ten minutes になると「ほかにある10分」、転じて「あと10分」。

155.「気楽に受けとれ」転じて「落ちつけ」という決まり文句。

156. making が分かりにくい場合は the smoke made に置き換えて、後半を別の文にしてみましょう。

157. Ed が knew したことは that 以下です。

158. as 以下は「時間」の付録で、「煙が clear な状態に向かい始めた時」。

p.50

"Ed!　What the hell are you doing!?" George shouted when he saw Ed take out a cutting knife.　A → B
"That pie isn't finished yet!"　A = B
But Ed cut the pie in half.　A → B
He broke off a piece of crust, dipped it in the filling, and popped it in his mouth.　A → B, (A) → B, and (A) → B
159. He tasted it for a moment and froze.　A → B and (A) ↩
Ed said something but the applause of the audience was getting louder and George couldn't hear him.　A → B but A = B and A → B

159. froze したのはエドです。

- 18 -

"Go," Jeremy said.　A→B

Ed nodded.　A↻

He started to run back but paused briefly only to say to Jeremy, "Thanks."　A→B but (A)↻

Jeremy closed his eyes again as Ed went dashing for the door.　A→B as A↻

146. He couldn't tell Ed who had messed with his stuff, and it hurt.　A→B／B', and A↻

147. It hurt very badly.　A↻

Ghost Avenue.　不完全な文

Same time.　不完全な文

Frank hurled piles of rotting magazines and pieces of wood into the fire, trying to warm up the theater.　A→B

148. But it was still cold.　A＝B

149. The cruel coldness sneaked in through the hole in the roof, the cracks in the wall, the broken windows, and anywhere else it could.　A↻

Willy had started shaking a few minutes ago.　A→B

150. BeeJees brought every rag he could find and wrapped them around Willy but the shaking didn't subside.
　　A→B and (A)→B but A↻

"Frank! More fire! Burn everything! Anything!" BeeJees shouted frantically.　A→B

Frank immediately took off his jacket and threw it into the fire.　A→B and (A)→B

151. But it was no use.　A＝B

"Prof!　不完全な文

Prof!　不完全な文

152. Hang on!　(A)↻

Stay with me, Prof!　(A)↻

153. That kid will be back soon with the money!　A＝B

I know he will!　A→B

Just hold on!"　(A)↻

Willy kept shaking.　A→B

BeeJees, tears in his eyes, hugged Willy from top of the blankets, trying to keep him from falling off the bed.
　　A→B

BeeJees was scared.　A＝B

146. ジェレミーは、エドの材料をすり替えた人物（who）をエドに打ち明けることができませんでした。it はそのことの代役です。

147. この It も犯人の正体を言えなかったことの代役です。

148. この it は気温を表す it。「時間」「気温」など、曖昧なものの代役は it におまかせです。

149. through 以下はすべて「場所」の付録。最後に anywhere（どこでも）と言っていますが、雰囲気を出すために具体的な場所も並べています。

150. he could find は rag の化粧文です。

151. it はフランクが火に投げ入れたジャケットの代役。しかし、「使い方がなかった」、転じて「役に立たなかった」。

152. 矢印の hang は「吊るす」「ぶらさがる」という言葉です。ウィリーは今まさに、命の淵にぶらさがっている状態です。hang on は定番中の定番の決まり文句で日本語の「がんばれ」に近い英語だと考えるとしっくりきます。苦しくても Hang on!（手を離すな！）

153. That kid とはエド。money はもちろんコンテストの賞金のこと。

p.44

"Wishbone!"　不完全な文

Ed stopped in the middle of the back alley when he heard his name.　A↺

Jeremy had appeared out of the shadows behind him.　A↺

139. In this damp, dark corridor, **all the music and excitement seemed** far away, as if it came from a different world.
A = B

Jeremy was alone.　A = B

He slowly **took** a few steps towards Ed.　A → B

Ed nervously **took** a step back.　A → B

140. **Jeremy Lightfoot Jr. wore** a solemn face.　A → B

He closed his eyes for a moment, **clenched** his fists, and just **stood** there.　A → B, (A) → B, and (A) ↺

141. **He seemed** like he was fighting something inside of himself.
A = B

"I... uh... have to go," **Ed said**, and **took** a step back towards his booth as Jeremy opened his mouth.
A → B, and (A) → B

"Check your pie," **Jeremy said**.　A → B

139. 再び「たとえ話」の as if です。音楽や歓声が different world からくるくらい遠くに感じられる、ということ。

140. 普段のジェレミーにはあまり見られない表情のため、wore（身につける）という矢印が使われています。

141. He は両方ジェレミーの代役。

p.45

"What?" **Ed asked**.　A → B

"Your pie.　不完全な文

142. **I saw someone mess with your supplies** when you weren't looking."　A → B = B'

Ed stared at Jeremy.　A → B

In the quiet refuge of the back alley, **the two young bakers** really **saw** each other for the first time.　A → B

143. And for some reason, **it seemed** like looking into a mirror.
A = B

144. **They** both **realized** it was not a matter of money or pride or proving anything anymore.　A → B

It was just about pies now.　A = B

"My pie?" **Ed whispered**, his face clouding.　A → B

Jeremy nodded.　A↺

142. 今回はよく出てくる mess という単語。stuff, guess などと並んで、口語ならではの曖昧な表現なので、いつでも使えて便利です。

143. it は前文 saw each other の代役。

144. it は、今二人が置かれている状況の代役。分かりにくければ、ずばり「戦う理由」と置き換えてみてください。でも、本当はもう少し曖昧にとらえる方が面白い文です。

p.46

Ed glanced at the clock on the wall.　A → B

There were only thirteen more minutes until time was up.
A = B

145. If something was wrong with the pie he was baking now, **there was** no time to start over again.　A = B

145. If からカンマまでの部分は、エドにとって、できれば想像したくない恐ろしい推測。もしそうなっていたら no time だとエドは考えています。

ビッグ・ファット・キャットの三色辞典

129. **"Did** my father **tell** you **to do this?"**   A→B／B'
   Billy Bob didn't **answer**.   A↻

   "Damn it!   (A)→B
130. **I'm not** going to let you and my father **mess** this up!   A＝B
131. **I'm** going to **win** this on my own!"   A＝B
   Billy Bob's cell phone **rang**.   A↻
   With one movement, **Billy Bob brushed** Jeremy aside and
      pulled his phone out.   A→B and (A)→B
   Jeremy went sprawling to the ground, hitting his elbow hard.
      A↻
   Ignoring Jeremy, **Billy Bob answered** the phone.   A→B
132. **Only Billy Bob's eyes kept** watching Jeremy, as if Jeremy too
      was a pet.   A→B
133. **"It's done," Billy Bob said** into the phone, then **hung up**.
      A→B, then (A)↻
   He **walked** away without any more words.   A↻
   Jeremy closed his eyes in both anger and bitterness.   A→B
   Back in the main arena, **the host continued** to feed the
      crowd's excitement.   A→B
   Upbeat music rocked the thin walls.   A→B
   The noise all **blended** together, erasing all sound, including
      the voice of Jeremy crying.   A↻

   "The clock now **reads** one-forty-five.   A→B
134. **Only fifteen minutes left!**   不完全な文
   "Most of the pies are already in the oven.   A＝B
135. **There's** a nice smell of sugar and spice in the air as I speak!
      A＝B
   Zombie Pies owner Jeremy Lightfoot Jr. disappeared
      mysteriously from his kitchen around the end of the first
      hour.   A↻
136. **We have** no information regarding Lightfoot's disappearance,
      but **it may be** part of some secret plan.   A→B, but A＝B
137. **"Meanwhile, Ed Wishbone and his assistant, now known to**
      the audience as 'the Tux,' have continued to hold the
      crowd's attention with their very unusual oven.   A→B
   "Oops, **it seems** for the moment, **Ed has disappeared** too.
      A＝B
138. **But I think** it's a safe guess that this has nothing to do with
      any secret plan."   A→B

131.「自分自身に寄り添って」、転じて「自分一人で」。on my own は決まり文句。

p.41

132. too は分かりにくければ取ってしまってもかまいません。

p.42

133. It が何の代役かは分かりません。どうやらビリー・ボブがエドの持ち物に何かをしたのはまちがいないようですが……。

134. 正しくは Only fifteen minutes are left.

135. おなじみの as 以下は、同時に起こっていることを表す「時間」の付録。

136. it は「Lightfoot's disappearance」の代役。

137. now から Tux まではアシスタント、つまりジョージの化粧品です。不似合いなタキシード姿を「The Tux」と軽い響きに略してからかわれています。

p.43

138. guess は英語では好んでよく使われる推測の言葉。日本語で「〜だと思う」という時に、英語では I guess という言い方をします。ここではアナウンサーが「safe（安全な）guess」と言っていますが、「当たる確率の高い安全な推測」として Ed's disappearance は secret plan とは無関係だろうと言っています。43 ページの挿絵を見ると、確かにそのようですが……。

Big Fat Cat's 3 Color Dictionary

p.39

The crowd **roared**. A↩

123. And from there on, **everything** became a blur.   A = B
The world **seemed** to move in fast-forward.   A = B
The battle **had begun**.   A↩

p.40

An hour later, Jeremy **was** about to finish his crust when he noticed Billy Bob standing near Ed Wishbone's booth.   A = B
Only Jeremy and a few others **could have** possibly **spotted** him.   A→B
He **was** standing in a shadowy corner.   A = B
A bad feeling **ran** through Jeremy's mind as **his busy hands stopped** moving for a moment.   A↩ as A→B

124. Billy Bob **was** checking to see if Ed Wishbone and his assistant were away from their table.   A = B

125. ── They **were**.   A = (B)
Ed and George **were** over by the barrel oven, trying to build up a steady fire.   A = B
Before Jeremy could even think, Billy Bob **stepped** out.   A↩
He **took** something from the table and **replaced** it with something else.   A→B and (A)→B

126. It **was** impossible to determine what it was, but he **had** definitely **done** something to Wishbone's materials.   A = B, but A→B

p.41

127. When Ed returned to his table a few seconds later, Billy Bob **had disappeared** completely, as if he had never been there.   A↩
Jeremy **took** off his apron and **laid** it on the table.
   A→B and (A)→B
He **hurried** out of the trailer and **went** racing through the back door.   A↩ and (A)↩
Billy Bob **was** just coming down the alley.   A = B
Enraged, Jeremy **confronted** Billy Bob head-on.   A→B
"You!   不完全な文
What **were** you doing?   A = B
Tell me!"   (A)→B
Jeremy **grabbed** Billy Bob by his jacket and **pulled**, but Billy Bob didn't move an inch.   A→B and (A)↩, but A↩

128. Nor **did** his expression **change**.   A↩

123. there はここでは物理的な場所ではなく、時間軸上の「場所」、つまりコンテストが始まった時刻。

124. checking to see は「チェックして見る」と考えてください。if 以下の文は「可能性」を表す文。ビリー・ボブは if 以下の可能性をチェックしています。

125. They は「エドとジョージ」の代役。強調のために中途半端に終わっていますが、後ろには前文の away が続きます。具体的な内容は次の文で。

126. 最初の It は to determine からカンマまでの代役。二番目の it はビリー・ボブのすりかえた「もの」の代役。

127. as if 以下はふつうの否定の文のようですが、ビリー・ボブは実際にはいたのですから、やはりこれもたとえ話です。「まるでなかったように」素早いビリー・ボブ。

128. 全体が否定の文です。書き直せば His expression did not change, either.

129. this は、ジェレミーが目撃したビリー・ボブの「怪しい行動すべて」の代役。

130. let という矢印は、何らかの希望を「かなえさせる」という意味の言葉。ここは否定の文なので、you（ビリー・ボブ）と father（ジェレミーの父）の希望を「かなえさせない」と言っているジェレミー。

"I didn't know Santa's beard was fake," George said in an
　　astonished face.　**A → B**
　Ed chuckled and turned back to his table.
　　A ↵ and (**A**) ↵
113. Everything was ready and in place.　**A = B**
　The only thing now was to decide what kind of pie to make.
　　A = B

114. Ed knelt down and inspected the bags he had brought.
　　A ↵ and (**A**) **→ B**
　In one bag were the ingredients for a blueberry pie.　**A = B**
　But the other bag held the ingredients for another kind of pie.
　　A → B
115. Ed had not mentioned this to George.　**A → B**
　The safe choice was blueberry.　**A = B**
　There was no doubt about it.　**A = B**
116. Yet, something inside Ed kept telling him that he should
　　enter the contest with his own pie.　**A → B**
117. Not a pie borrowed from his mother's recipe book.　不完全な文
118. But that was risky.　**A = B**
　It was more than a risk.　**A = B**
　Yet...　不完全な文
　His hand was moving slowly towards the second bag when
　　George said,　**A = B**
　"Damn!　不完全な文
119. Willy sure would have wanted to see this!"　**A → B**

　Ed's hand stopped a few inches from the bag.　**A ↵**
　He clenched the hand into a fist, then grabbed the bag with
　　the blueberries in it instead.　**A → B**, (**A**) **→ B**
　Willy.　不完全な文
　Ed thought to himself.　**A ↵**
　Think about Willy.　(**A**) **→ B**
120. You have to win.　**A → B**
121. No matter what.　不完全な文
122. Moments later, the bell rang again, and all of the contestants
　　sprang to a start.　**A ↵**, and **A ↵**
　The clock tower standing in the middle of the tent turned
　　twelve.　**A ↵**
　The host was shouting in excitement.　**A = B**

p.37

p.38

113. in place は「あるべき場所にある」という意味。

114. he 以下は bags の化粧文。

115. this は前の文の内容の代役。

116. エドの内側の何かが that 以下の思いを語りかけてきます。

117. 前文の his own pie をもっと具体的に説明しています。borrowed 以下は pie の化粧品。

118. that は 2 つ前の文の「エドの思い」通りに行動することの代役。

119. sure は強調の言葉。this はこの華やかな大舞台。

120. 「勝つことを（予定の中に）持っている」、転じて「勝たなければならない」。エドが自分に言い聞かせています。

p.39

121. 「何があろうとも」という決まり文句。what は「起こり得るあらゆる種類の問題すべて」の代役。勝つためにはどんな問題もみんな no matter（関係ない）になってしまいます。

122. sprang は spring の変形した形。spring は「春」ではなく、「バネ（スプリング）」の方の spring。その矢印バージョンです。

p.35

103. **Ed looked** up from the table as Santa took off his beard.   A↺
     It **was** the owner of the New Mall.   A = B

103.顔からあごひげを off すると、その下から現れたのは……。

p.36

104. "Ed Wishbone! I thought that was you!" **the owner said**.   A→B

     "**I was** worried after you disappeared from the clinic.   A = B
     Are you okay?"   A = B
     Ed smiled awkwardly as he replied.   A↺
     "I'm fine, sir.   A = B
     I'm sorry for everything.   A = B

104. that はオーナーが遠くから見たエドの姿。

105. **I don't** really **remember** much about that night."   A→B
     "No problem, no problem," **the owner said**, but **the smile faded** from his face.   A→B, but A↺

105. that night は『ビッグ・ファット・キャット、街へ行く』での一夜のこと。

106. "You know, **Jeremy Lightfoot's bodyguard came** to my office several days after you disappeared.   A↺
     He had a paper with your signature on it.   A→B

106. several 以下は「時間」の付録。

107. **It said** that you disclaimed all rights to the space in the Food Court.   A→B
     I **knew** the paper was suspicious, but I really **had** no choice but to believe it."   A→B, but A→B
     Ed nodded.   A↺
     "So I **didn't rent** the space to Zombie Pies either.   A→B

107. It は「エドが無理矢理サインをさせられた紙」の代役。

108. Instead, **I saved** it as the prize for the contest today.
     A→B = B'
     I sincerely **hope** you win."   A→B

108. it は、結局オーナーが誰の手にも渡さなかった「space in the Food Court」の代役。space は最終的に as 以下のようになりました。

p.37

     "**Thank** you."   (A)→B
     "**I'm** sorry about what happened."   A = B
     "No.   不完全な文
109. **Don't be**.   不完全な文

109. 2文前の I'm sorry を受けた Don't be sorry. をここではこう略しています。

110. **It was** all for the best.   A = B
     I..."   不完全な文

110.「すべてはベストの結果のために動いていた」という、大変前向きな言い回し。

111. Just then, **a bell rang** throughout the main tent, signaling the start of the contest in five minutes.   A↺
112. **The owner** hurriedly **put** his beard back on.   A→B
     He smiled at Ed.   A↺
     "Good luck, Mr. Wishbone."   不完全な文
     "Thank you, sir," **Ed said**.   A▸B
     The owner ran off, his fluffy cap flip-flopping with every step.
     A↺

111. in five minutes はこれからの5分間がすべて「現在」という時間の内側にのみこまれた (in になった) 状態、つまり「5分後」のこと。

112.何に on したかというと、his face にです。

The carrier **rolled** over twice and **the door of the cage sprang** wide open. A↶ and A↶

95. **Everything lay** still for a while. A↶
96. But then, inch by inch, **Mr. Jones pushed its head** out and **looked** around. A→B and (A)→B
— After a brief pause, **Mr. Jones hid** inside the cage again. A↶

Another minute passed. A↶
Mr. Jones decided to take a step outside again. A→B
It slowly **crept** out of the cage, and even more slowly, **took one step, then two steps** out on the ground.
A↶, and (A)→B

97. **It felt** good. A↶
Mr. Jones took a big stretch and **narrowed its eyes**.
A→B and (A)→B
It then **walked** over to a trailer tire, **sniffed it**, and **rubbed a side** against it. A↶, (A)→B, and (A)→B
Satisfied, **Mr. Jones continued** walking down the alley. A→B

98. **It couldn't understand** what was happening, but **being outside of the cage was** much **better** than being inside of it. A→B, but A=B

99. **Free space to walk around was luxurious**. A=B
100. *So this was the world outside*. A=B
The world beyond the bars. 不完全な文

It was so free, and... A=B

... and it was also pretty scary. A=B

101. **The last time George had seen a real Santa Claus was more than thirty years ago, back in elementary school**. A=B
His mom had taken all the kids to the Outside Mall one afternoon, where Santa came every winter. A→B
102. **Back then, the Outside Mall was the coolest place a kid could go**. A=B
Now, thirty years later, **a chubby Santa with a white beard and red suit was walking** straight towards them. A=B
"Ed Wishbone?" **Santa Claus asked**. A→B
George turned to Ed, his eyes wide open. A↶
"You're friends with Santa?" **George asked**. A→B

---

p.32

95.分かりにくければ lay を was に換えて読んでみてください。この still は「静かな」。

96. inch by inch は「1インチずつ」、つまり「ほんのちょっとずつ」という表現。

97.この it は今の状況全体の代役ですが、Mr. Jones の代役として読むことも可能です。

98.最初の It は Mr. Jones の代役。最後の it はかごの代役です。「かごの中」と「かごの外」を比べています。

99.飼い猫 Mr. Jones にとってのぜいたく、それは「自由に歩ける空間」。

100. So は文のはじめに単独で使われると、「なるほど、そうか」というニュアンスの出だしになります。

p.33
p.34
p.35

101. The last time は「(ジョージが本物のサンタを見た) 最後の時」。real が化粧品としてサンタについているあたりが実にジョージらしいところ。

102.Back は時間を語る時にも「後ろ」の方、つまり過去を指します。cool という言葉はあらゆる年齢、性別、人種を超えて、英語の口語のほめ言葉で最高クラスの「かっこいい」を指します。

p.30

He slowly **pulled** his hand back and **hid** it behind him.
    A→B and (A)→B
It **hurt**. A↩
"I **said**... quiet. A→B
85. **Stop** laughing, and **keep** your mind on your job."
    (A)→B, and (A)→B = B'
86. The surprised assistant **replied**, "Yes, sir." A→B
He **got** back to work in a hurry. A↩
87. Jeremy **glanced** at Ed and George with a look of disgust,
    then **focused** again on his oven. A→B, then (A)→B
88. He **tried** to dismiss the duo from his mind, but **kept**
    remembering the taste of that pie. A→B, but (A)→B
An ordinary pie. 不完全な文
That **was** *all*. A = B
An ordinary fruit pie. 不完全な文
But he still **couldn't forget** the taste. A→B
It **made** him **nervous**. A→B = B'
"Okay, Wishbone. You're here," Jeremy **mumbled**. A→B
89. "Now, **prove** yourself." (A)→B

85.「意識を仕事にくっつけておけ」、転じて「仕事に集中しろ」。

86. surprised は assistant の化粧品です。いつもと違うジェレミーにアシスタントは当惑気味。

87. with からカンマまでは「どのように」の付録。

88. the duo はエドとジョージの代役で「二人組」を指します。that pie はエドの作ったパイ。ジェレミーが前話でぶつけられたあのパイです。

89. 以前にもジェレミーがエドに言ったことのあるセリフ。いよいよエドが「自らを証明する時」が来ました。

p.31

Meanwhile behind the Zombie Pies trailer. 不完全な文
90. Billy Bob **listened** to his cell phone in silence. A→B
He **didn't say** anything. A→B
He **didn't** even nod. A↩
He just **listened**. A↩
Finally, before hanging up, he **said** one phrase. A→B
"Yes, sir." 不完全な文
91. Billy Bob **was standing** between the trailer and the back wall
    where almost nobody could see him. A = B
He carefully **set** Mr. Jones' carrier cage down on the ground
    and **moved** away into the back alley. A→B and (A)↩
A moment later, Jeremy's assistant **came** rushing out of the
    trailer. A↩
92. Jeremy **was yelling**, "Go get it and hurry!" from behind him.
    A = B
93. The assistant **was** so **upset** that he **swung** open the back
    door with all of his might. A = B that A→B
94. The door **hit** Mr. Jones' cage and **knocked** it over.
    A→B and (A)→B

90. cellular phone の略。携帯電話の英語での一般的な呼び方。

91. where 以下は「場所」の付録で、ビリー・ボブが今いるのがどんなところか説明しています。

92. it が何の代役かは不明ですが、パイに使う何かであることはまちがいありません。him は走って行くアシスタントの代役です。

93. with 以下は「どのように」の付録で、「力の限り」という意味の言い回し。

94. it は Mr. Jones' cage の代役。

76. Let's see... his name seems to be 'Ed Wishbone.'   A = B
77. Funny, the name sort of rings a bell.   A → B
    Where have I heard...   A ↺
    Holy cow!   不完全な文
    It's the baker from Ghost Avenue!   A = B
    We've all seen him on the six o'clock news!   A → B
    My God, I don't want to be rude here, but Ed, man, maybe you should open your eyes and take a look around!
    A → B, but A → B and (A) → B

    "Uh-oh... More bad news.   不完全な文
    I'm afraid Mr. Tuxedo here is Ed's assistant.   A = B (that) A = B
78. I just hope that barrel he's dragging isn't what I think it is.
    A → B
79. If this is a joke, it sure seems to work, because everyone in the stands is laughing like crazy.   A = B
80. Ladies and gentlemen, let's just hope that the judges' health is still intact when they go home tonight!"   (A) → B

    "Holy macaroni! Is that his oven!?" Jeremy's assistant said.
    A → B
    He was laughing and pointing at Ed as they set up the barrel oven.   A = B
81. George was so embarrassed that he lost his grip, and the barrel oven toppled over.   A = B that A → B, and A ↺
82. The crowd went wild.   A ↺
    Ed and George just kept on trying to balance the barrel.
    A → B
83. The crowd laughed as if they were watching a circus.   A ↺
    "Is he really going to enter the contest!?   A = B
84. Man, talk about crazy people..."   (A) → B
    "Shut up," Jeremy said.   A → B
    He was concentrating on checking the oven.   A = B
    "But boss, you should take a look at this guy.   A → B
    He is totally out of his..."   A = B

    Jeremy hit the top of the oven hard with his hand.   A → B
    The assistant stopped babbling.   A → B
    Jeremy was dressed in costume, but his face was dead serious.   A = B, but A = B

---

p.27

考え、その左右がそれぞれAの箱とBの箱と考えます。what I think it is は全部で「思い浮かべているアレ」。「まさかアレがオーブンじゃないよな」と司会者は hope しています。

p.28

79. ドラム缶はジョークのための道具として work しているようです。ここでの crazy も肯定的なイメージです。

80. hope していることは that 以下。

81. 「grip をなくす」転じて「握りしめたこぶしをゆるめる」。当然握っていたオーブンは toppled してしまいます。

p.29

82. ここでの wild も crazy と極めて近い意味で使われています。wild とはもともと「野性的」という意味の言葉ですが、日常に登場する場合は「野生のように」転じて「むちゃくちゃに」という意味で使われがちです。一般的に crazy よりも激しい状態を指しています。

83. as if 以下は「まるで○○しているみたいに」というたとえ話です。

84. これもよくある言い回しです。省略せずに書くと、Man, we talk about crazy people, but he sure is one.「crazy な人がいるとは言うけれど」とあきれた感じを出しています。ここでの crazy が肯定的か否定的かは解釈次第。

p.30

George looked at Ed with big, frightened-puppy eyes. A→B
67. George was probably the only person in the whole festival grounds wearing a tuxedo, except for the stuffed bear on the counter of a nearby booth. A=B
"This is crazy, man. A=B
BeeJees is right. A=B
68. We're waaaay out of our league here. A=B
Let's go home." (A)↩
George turned to leave, but Ed grabbed his arm.
   A↩, but A→B
69. "George, we've got no choice." A→B
"I know, man. A↩
But I'm scared." A=B
"Me too," Ed said, and started walking towards the main tent. A→B, and (A)→B
George stood there alone at the gate for a moment. A↩
But when people nearby began to look at him suspiciously, he started to run after Ed — but fell because of his shaking legs. A→B but (A)↩
He got up and continued to run. A↩ and (A)→B
"Ed! 不完全な文
Hey! 不完全な文
Wait up! (A)↩
Ed!" 不完全な文
70. Unnoticed by either of them, a dark shadow crouched by the gate silently, watching everything. A↩

71. "Thank you, Glen. (A)→B
And now, this is your host Robert R. Silverman from inside the main tent. A=B
Almost all of the contestants have finished setting up their kitchens here on the battleground. A→B
72. All we can do is wait for the clock to... oops, someone just came into the tent from the contestant's side. A=B, A↩
73. "Hey, mister, you've got the wrong gate! A→B
But, oh... wait a minute... am I dreaming this, or...
   (A)→B... A=B
Good Lord! 不完全な文
74. This man seems to be our last contestant! A=B
75. "He has now stopped at booth five. A↩

67. ジョージと同じ格好をしているのは……24 ページの挿絵を探してみてください。

68. waaaay はもちろんミスプリントではありません。ここでの way は away の省略された形で、「ずっと遠く」という意味。本当に遠いのを強調するためにジョージがのばして発音しています。

69. no choice で「選択肢がない」。

70. them はエドとジョージの代役です。

71. テレビのレポーターがコンテストの司会者に替わり、中継場所もテントの中に移りました。

72. エドが someone と表現されているのは、とてもコンテスト参加者に見えなかったため。

73. 司会者は、エドたちをお客さんだと勘ちがいしている様子。

74. seems だけでなく、seems to be までをすべてイコールと考えると分かりやすくなります。

75. He はエドの代役。

76. Let us see. の略。「見てみよう」という意味ですが、ニュアンスとしては「どれどれ」というようなしゃべり始めの置き言葉です。

77. ここでの Funny は首をかしげるような「おかしさ」。

78. that 以下の文は、isn't をイコールとして

ビッグ・ファット・キャットの三色辞典

58. **The crowd is** going crazy!   A＝B
　　We now **present** you, the one and only... ZOMBIE PIES!!
　　A→B／B'

　　"**It's** the strangest pie shop in the history of strange pie shops!   A＝B
　　The Pie God himself, Jeremy Lightfoot Jr., and the colorful Zombie Pies trailer **are** now **entering** the tent.   A＝B
59. Their horrifying mascot, 'The Gravedigger,' **stalks** the grounds while the 'Grim Zombies' are scaring kids who unfortunately got in their way!   A→B
　　Already condemned by twenty-one school boards, Zombie Pies **is** nevertheless the most famous pie shop in ten surrounding states!   A＝B
　　"Reporting live from the entrance of the PIEGAMES, **I'm** Glen Hamperton!   A＝B
　　The battle **is** about to begin!!"   A＝B

　　Meanwhile... at the main gate.   不完全な文
　　"Oh my God..." George **said**, and **forgot** to shut his mouth.
　　A→B, and (A)→B
60. "Ed, I **think** this is a big mistake."   A→B
　　George **stared** at the fabulous Zombie Pies trailer truck as it entered the tent, his mouth wide open.   A→B
61. Ed **was** also **frozen** there at the gate of the pie festival.   A＝B
　　He **scanned** the festival grounds with both his eyes, surprised at how big the event was.   A→B
62. There **was** a Ferris wheel standing at the far side, along with several other carnival rides.   A＝B

63. **Countless** booths selling every kind of pie on earth **were** lined back to back down the main area.   A＝B
64. People of all ages **were** everywhere.   A＝B
　　There **were** balloons, flags, and other multi-colored decorations all around.   A＝B
65. Before arriving at the festival grounds, Ed **had imagined** an auditorium with fifty or a hundred people.   A→B
66. He **couldn't have been** more wrong.   A＝B
　　Ed **gulped**.   A↩

ます。ここでも「狂ったように喜んでいる」という肯定のイメージで使われています。   p.22

59. grounds は「地面」ですが、ここではその「一帯」を指しています。who 以下は kids の化粧文ですが、難しければ読み飛ばしてしまっても大丈夫。their way は「Zombies の通り道」のこと。   p.23

60. this は「エドたちがコンテストに出場すること」の代役。

61. frozen は「凍ったような状態」を表します。

62. エドとジョージがいるゲートから見て far side に観覧車があります。far という言葉に会場の広さを感じてみてください。   p.24

63. selling から earth までは booths の化粧品で、「地球上の全種類のパイを売っている」という少し大げさな表現。読み飛ばしても文は通じます。back to back は「背中合わせ」。

64. all ages で「すべての年齢」。

65. エドが想像していた会場とは、だいぶ様子がちがっていたようです。   p.25

66. 少し矛盾した言葉遊びです。「これ以上もっとまちがう」ことが不可能なぐらいまちがっていた、ということで、エドの勘ちがいの度合いを際立たせています。

p.19

"Ai-ya!" Frank replied.   A→B

George was waiting by the doors, dressed in his best outfit.   A＝B

It was a cheap tuxedo.   A＝B

49. He looked like a boy waiting for his first day of Sunday school.   A＝B
50. This made Ed smile again.   A→B＝B'

"Ed," BeeJees suddenly shouted.   A→B

51. Ed looked back as BeeJees threw him a fortune cookie.   A↩ as A→B／B'

Ed caught the cookie with both hands.   A→B

52. "Take Willy with you," BeeJees said.   A→B

Ed raised his eyes and nodded once.   A→B and (A)↩

53. It was time to go.   A＝B

p.20

"This is Glen Hamperton, reporting from outside the main tent of the State Pie Festival.   A＝B

54. The time is now ten a.m. and contestants should be here any minute now... and YES!   A＝B and A＝B

Here they come!   A↩

This year's pie warriors!   不完全な文

55. "Leading the group is the two-time contest winner 'Brown Butters' — now at four locations around the state.   A＝B

Their famous 'Brown Butter Vanilla Double Crust' has been the number one best-selling pie for more than fifteen years!   A＝B

p.21

56. "Right behind them are the 'Buffi Brothers.'   A＝B

Combining traditional Italian cuisine with the art of pie baking, they have created a revolution in the history of pies.   A→B

Their specialty is the 'Pepperoni Pie' with cheese, tomato sauce, pasta and a whole lot of sliced pepperoni!   A＝B

p.22

"And... oh my God... what is that blue smoke back there!?   A＝B

Has there been an accident?   A＝B

No, wait... that music, that rhythm... Yes, everyone!   不完全な文

57. This is the one you've been waiting for!   A＝B

---

49. Sunday school は子供たちが日曜日に行く教会学校。たいてい一番いい服を着て出かけるのですが、スーツなどは立派すぎて、かえって奇妙に見えてしまいます。

50. This は前文全体の代役。

51. as の前の文と後ろの文がほぼ同時に起こっています。

52. さすがにウィリー本人を連れて行くことはできないので、代わりに、ということです。

53. 「go する時間」転じて「出発の時」。

54. any minute は「いつでも」という時間の付録。

55. A の箱の中身を The leader of the group にすると分かりやすくなります。この time は「回数」を表す time。

56. them は「Brown Butters（のスタッフたち）」の代役。

57. the one は本来 the one pie shop。you've 以下はその化粧文です。the one の正体が何かというと……まもなく分かるはずです。

58. 「狂った」という悪い意味の言葉だった crazy ですが、現代のアメリカではむしろ「狂ったようにすごい」を含めた誉め言葉のイメージが強くなってい

40. "The Prof loved these things. A→B
41. The Chinese store downtown used to give him cookies that had expired. A→B／B'
    He cracked one open every morning and read the paper inside. A→B＝B' and (A)→B
42. It always said something stupid like that. A→B
    He just read them and smiled. A→B and (A)↩
43. That crazy old bastard." 不完全な文
    BeeJees laughed weakly. A↩
    Ed had taken his bandanna out and was folding it in half.
    A→B and (A)＝B
    He wrapped it around his head and tied it in the back.
    A→B and (A)→B
44. Right then, Frank came rolling around the corner in his toy wagon. A↩
    He said "Howdy" to Ed and waved at him. A→B and (A)↩
    Ed waved back. A↩
    "You really think you can win this contest?" BeeJees asked.
    A→B
    Ed held a solemn expression on his face, but his eyes were determined. A→B, but A＝B
    BeeJees cracked open another fortune cookie. A→B＝B'
    This time, he crushed it without even reading the paper inside. A→B
    "Do you at least have a plan? A→B
    Everyone else in the contest is a professional. A＝B
    You're just a guy from a small town. A＝B
    What do you plan to do?" A→B
    "What Willy told me." 不完全な文
45. Ed reached for his bag as he said, "Try to be a baker."
    A→B

    Ed started for the door, looking back at Willy one last time.
    A↩
46. Willy slept on, cuddled in a pile of dirty rags. A↩
    At least he deserves a better bed, Ed thought. A→B
47. It made him want to cry. A→B＝B'
    But there was no time for crying. A＝B
48. "Watch the cat for me, Frank. It's going to be a disaster if the cat finds out where I'm going," Ed said to Frank. A→B

---

p.18

ページに出てくる「笑い」のひとつで、「クックックッ」といった無音の笑いのこと。

40. these things はフォーチュンクッキーの代役。things はなんでも「もの」というひとくくりに含めてしまう言葉のため、少し投げやりな響きがあります。ビージーズにしてみれば「こんなもの」という気持ちでの言葉。

41. used to は懐かしく過去を回想するときに使います。that 以下は cookies の化粧文。

42. that は、ビージーズがさっき読み上げた運勢。

43. bastard はもともと「ひどい人間」に対して使う悪口。照れ屋のビージーズはここではウィリーに対して、愛情を込めて使っています。old はただ「古い」という意味でなく、どこか「愛すべき古さ」という温もりも持っている単語。

44. Right then は「その時」。

45. 完全な文にすると、I will try to be a baker. になります。

p.19

46. on は何かに接触している状態。「寝るという行為」に接触している状態なので、転じて「寝続ける」。

47. It は前文全体の代役。

48. if 以下は「可能性」を表す文。もしも if 以下が起こったら、「大災害になる」と大げさに心配するエド。

p.16

The street **was** still quiet.   A = B
It **was** nearly nine a.m., but in Ghost Avenue, **morning was** longer than any other place.   A = B, but, A = B
Ed **crept** through the piles of junk inside the Old Everville Cinema, heading towards the campfire in the middle.   A ↻
29. BeeJees **was** half-asleep near the fire.   A = B
30. Besides him, Willy **lay** on a fake bed that Ed and the others had made.   A ↻
31. Willy **hadn't woken** up once in two days.   A ↻
32. He **was** still alive, but barely.   A = B
"Willy," Ed **whispered**.   A → B
But Willy **didn't react**.   A ↻
33. "I **have** to go. But I'll **be** back soon. Then we'll **get** you to a hospital, okay?" Ed **said**.   A → B
The light of the fire **fell** on Willy's face.   A ↻
34. Sometimes the flickering light **made** Willy **seem** to move a little.   A → B = B'
Unfortunately, it **was** always only a trick of the eye.   A = B

p.17

A faint cracking sound **broke** the silence.   A → B
35. Ed **looked** behind him and **found** BeeJees **awake**, slumped against an old sign.   A ↻ and (A) → B = B'
36. BeeJees **was** holding a fortune cookie which he had just cracked open in his hands.   A = B
37. "BeeJees, I'm sorry about what I said the other night," Ed **said** to BeeJees.   A → B
"I... I'm really sorry."   A = B
BeeJees **scratched** his head, **frowned**, and **looked** down.
   A → B, (A) ↻, and (A) ↻
He **pulled** out a thin piece of paper from inside the fortune cookie.   A → B
After a long pause, he **read** from the paper in a flat voice.
   A → B
38. "*There* **are** *chances, and there* **are** *consequences*."
   A = B, and A = B
39. BeeJees **shook** his head and **chuckled**.   A → B and (A) ↻
"What the hell **does** that **mean**?"   A → B

p.18

He **dropped** the paper and cookie on the floor and **crushed** them under his foot.   A → B and (A) → B

---

29. half をつければたいていのものは効力を若干失います。きっちり半分ということではなく、かなり曖昧に「半分」です。ここでは「眠りかけていた」。

30. that 以下は bed の化粧文。

31. 否定の文。前話のラストから 2 日が経っています。

32. 再び barely。生と死の境目で「ちょっとだけ」生きている側にいるウィリーです。

33. you はウィリーの代役。「ウィリーをとって、病院へ向かう」、転じて「ウィリーを病院へ連れて行く」。

34. seem to がついているのでそのあとの move a little はそう見えただけ。

35. awake 以下はビージーズの状態。

36. フォーチュンクッキーは中華料理の焼き菓子で、固いクッキーの中に運勢が書かれた紙切れが入ったもの（18 ページの挿絵参照）。which 以下は cookie の化粧文です。

37. the other night は「(今日じゃない) ほかの夜」。転じて、「この前の夜」。前話で病院に出発する直前に言ってしまったことをエドは謝っています。

38. consequence は「結果」ですが、「悪い結果」という方にかなり強く偏った言葉です。同じ結果でも result の方がどちらかといえば中立的です。

39. chuckle は解説 59

19. **"Let's get** going.**"** (A) → B
    "You're damn right, we're going!" George shouted as he
       stood up in pride. A → B
20. And with that, the day began. A ↩
21. "AAAAND IT'S A GREAT NEW DAY!! A = B
    The balloons are up! A = B
22. We're on top of the New Everville Mall this morning,
       reporting live from the annual State Pie Festival! A = B
23. This is Glen Hamperton, bringing you the excitement below
       — live on the morning news!" A = B

"Today, eighteen shops and individuals enter the pie contest
   to find the best pie in the state. A → B
This year's main sponsor Wilson Artwill, the owner of the
   New Everville Mall, has prepared a huge cash prize of
   twenty thousand dollars and a free space for a shop in
   his Food Court. A → B
"The rules are simple. A = B
24. Contestants have two hours to bake the best pie. A → B
    They can use any ingredients they choose, but each
       contestant can have only one assistant for help.
       A → B, but A → B

"At the end of two hours, all the pies will be presented to the
   judges. A = B
25. Each contestant will introduce their pie in the way they wish.
       A → B
    After tasting all eighteen pies, the judges will each vote
       for the best pie. A → B
26. The numbers will be added up, and the single contestant
       with the highest score will win the 'GOLDEN CRUST'
       trophy along with the prize money and the store space!
       A = B and A → B
    The excitement is heating up as the time draws near for the
       battle of the pies to begin! A = B as A ↩
27. "WELCOME TO THE PIEGAMES! 不完全な文
    "I'm Glen Hamperton reporting live from the air above
       Everville! A = B
28. See you later, folks!" (A) → B

---

19. Let's は Let us の省略形ですが、このようにひとつの矢印と考えてもかまいません。「going (行くこと) をとる」で、転じて「出発しよう」。これもよくある言い回し。

20. that はこのシーン全部ととらえても、直前のジョージのセリフととらえてもかまいません。

21. 英語には音をのばす記号がないので、こういった表現が用いられることがあります。

22. top は、Mall の top、つまり上空。同時に精神的な高揚感も表しています。

23. below は上空から見た眼下のモール。

24. to 以下は何をするための2時間かを具体的に説明しています。

25. in 以下は「どのように」の付録ですが、ある意味、「場所」の付録ともいえます。「望む道の中で」、転じて「好きな方法で」。

26. numbers はここでは「得票数」。

27. PIEGAMES はこの大会のために作られた造語。game は「競う要素」がある遊び全般に用いられますが、真剣な戦いの場合にも、少しユーモアをこめて使うことがあります。

28. folks という呼びかけは群衆を相手に気軽に話しかける時に使います。

p.11
p.12
p.14
p.15

p.10

9. "George, you can't sit in the front row today," he said to George. A→B
   "Oh..."   不完全な文
   A look of despair crossed George's face for a moment. A→B
   But he replied quickly.   A↩
10. He was used to this kind of treatment all his life. A=B
    "Oh... well, I know.   A↩
11. I guess I would make a bad impression on the judges. A→B
    Hey, no problem!   不完全な文
    I'll just stay in the back and keep..."   A↩ and (A)↩
    Ed held the contest flier out to George.   A→B
12. An entry form and a list of rules were printed on the back.
    A=B
    Ed pointed to one particular rule.   A→B

9. 今日のパイ・コンテスト会場でのこと。

10. this kind of treatment はエドがジョージにとった、一見冷たい態度のこと。

11. Bの箱の中をさらに色分けすると、I would make a bad impression on the judges. ホームレスが最前列で like hell に応援していたら、確かに審査員に好印象ではないはず。

12. ここでの back はチラシの「裏」。

p.11

13. "It says here, I can bring one assistant."   A→B
    Ed smiled.   A↩
    "You're going to be that assistant."   A=B
14. "Say what?" George replied.   A→B
15. His face turned red as he looked up at Ed.   A↩
    He immediately shook his head.   A→B
16. "No way, man.   不完全な文
    You don't want me!   A→B
    Uh-un!   不完全な文
    I'll just mess things up.   A→B
17. I always do."   A↩
    "I went to the Mall yesterday and registered. You already are my assistant, George. I need your help," Ed said.   A→B
    George stared at Ed.   A→B
    The morning sun, now higher in the sky, gave bright light onto the old neighborhood.   A→B
    Most of the others were still asleep and the street was quiet.
    A=B and A=B
    "Are you sure?" George asked.   A→B
    Ed nodded.   A↩
18. "Nobody ever asked for my help. Ed... you're... you're so..."
    George said in a trembling voice.   A→B
    "Come on, George," Ed said, looking up into the blue sky.
    A→B
    It seemed to be the start of a really nice winter day.   A=B

13. It はチラシの代役。ここでの say は「表記されている」ということ。

14. 本来は "What did you say?"。少し砕けた言い回しです。

15. turn は何かがクルッと一瞬で様子を変える時に使う矢印です。

16. No way は決まり文句で、「そんな道（自分がアシスタントになる道）なんてない」、転じて「それはあり得ない」。

17. do は前文の矢印 mess の代役。mess の正確なニュアンスは「ぐちゃぐちゃにする」。

18. shake も tremble も「ふるえる」ですが、tremble の方がより小刻みなふるえです。

"George..." 不完全な文
"George..." 不完全な文
"It's morning." A = B

"Oh... Ed. Good morning," George said. A → B
1. He rubbed his sleepy eye with one hand as he got up. A → B
2. The sun was barely up in the sky. A = B
Fresh and crisp air filled the dawn of Everville's older streets. A → B
It was seven o'clock in the morning — the beginning of a new day. A = B
After a moment of recovery, George smiled and pointed before him. A ↩ and (A) → B
3. "There's your stuff. A = B
Good and ready." 不完全な文

In front of George, there was a pile of kitchen utensils that Ed used everyday. A = B
4. They were the cheapest brand at the nearby supermarket, but now they shined like silver in the morning light. A = B, but A ↩
Ed noticed that George's hands were all red. A → B
5. "This was all I could do. But I'll be in the front row today, cheering like hell," George said. A → B
Ed picked up his rolling pin. A → B
Yesterday, it had been an old gray color. A = B
Now it was practically new. A = B
"George... we don't have any sandpaper. A → B
This is impossible. A = B
How did you..." 不完全な文
George took out a completely worn-out toothbrush. A → B
He grinned like a child. A ↩
Ed stood amazed. A ↩
6. He couldn't imagine how many hours it would take to scrub a rolling pin with a toothbrush. A → B
"George, this is impossible!" A = B
7. "Almost," George said and smiled. A → B and (A) ↩

Ed touched the rolling pin with the tip of his fingers. A → B
8. He thought he could feel the warmth inside. A → B

ビッグ・ファット・キャットの三色辞典

p.7

p.8

1.二つの文が as で結ばれている形は大変よく出てきます。as 以下の2つ目の文は本来は同時に起こっていることを示す「時間」の付録ですが、単純に二つの文が同時に起こっていると考えることもできます。三色辞典中では難しい文に限って、二つの文として色分けしています。

2. barely と almost は似た意味の言葉ですが、almost は「少し足りない状態」で、barely は「少し超えた状態」です。ここではbarely なので、太陽はわずかに顔を出しています。

p.9

3.stuff は名前のないものをひとまとめに表現する時に使う便利な言葉です。似た意味の単語として 18 ページにもうひとつ things が出てきます。

4.cheap は単に「安い」というよりも、「安かろう悪かろう」のマイナスイメージがある言葉です。nearby は「近隣の」。

5.all I could do は「自分ができることすべて」。

6.エドが imagine できなかったのは、to scrub 以下のジョージがやったことにかかった時間。

7.「少し足りない状態」を示す almost。「危なく不可能だったよ」とジョージは得意気。

8.rolling pin の inside です。

p.10

BIG FAT CAT'S
3 COLOR DICTIONARY

BIG FAT CAT
VS.
MR. JONES